Building a Business to Last

Simple Success Strategies for the
Small Business Start-Up

CONTENTS

Part One - Customers and Relationships

Part Two - Effective and Efficient Communication

Part Three - Avoiding Miscommunication and Conflict

Introduction

Do you own your own business or dream of having a successful business?

I've owned my business for more than twenty-eight years and have learned many lessons the hard way. I've written this book to show you how to be more successful and profitable in your business by building and keeping great customer relationships through service and communication. You don't need to learn all business lessons the hard way.

If you are a business owner, you may think you should be making more money from your efforts. Are you putting in long hours and not seeing the profits you feel you deserve and have earned? Maybe you feel as if your customers are a pain in the neck, or worse. You may believe your customers don't understand how hard you work and how difficult your job is. You're right: Most customers don't understand and never will.

Insight and instruction in communication and service will be of great help to you. None of us want to learn everything through trial and error— that's financially and emotionally draining.

What you will learn from this book:

- ♦ How to make more money.
- ♦ How to gain repeat and referral customers through relationships.
- ♦ How to communicate more clearly with customers.
- ♦ How to give exceptional service at no extra cost to you.
- ♦ How to avoid misunderstandings.

- How to work with an angry customer and keep your sanity.
- How to think through problems easily.
- Pitfalls to avoid.

This book is written in simple, straightforward language; it's an easy read. Knowledge is presented in a way that makes sense. Vague business ideas and theories have been avoided. You will find true-life examples throughout of the principles discussed. Useful, practical knowledge that increases your profitability and can be put to use immediately is within these pages.

PART ONE

Customer Relationships and Service

CHAPTER 1

A Business's Most Critical Asset

Being a successful business owner of any size business is one of the most challenging yet incredibly rewarding positions to be in. It's a journey of self discovery. At the start of our business journey we aren't fully aware of that fact.

Most days we are juggling a multitude of responsibilities, running from one task to another, trying desperately to get everything done, to meet all our obligations, and to make everyone happy. Boredom is never an issue; there are always new demands and challenges to be met. Some challenges and problems are unnecessary, unwanted, and unrewarding. Sometimes our lack of knowledge and understanding, along with poor habitual behavior, results in our creating problems for ourselves.

What are some of these problems that blindside you and waste your precious time? Doesn't time mean money in business? You bet it does. Unhappy, upset, complaining customers take a huge chunk of our time, not to mention our mental and emotional energy. You probably spend more time and energy with an unhappy customer than with a satisfied customer. Wouldn't it be heaven if most of your customers were happy with the service and products they received?

All of us in business are in it to make money. If not, then it's a hobby. There are many reasons to be a business owner: Loving what you do, pride of ownership, and being your own boss, just to name a few. The harsh reality is that we have to make money to stay in business and to make a living or we will not be business owners for long.

Statistics tell us that most small businesses fail after five years. 2008 statistics on the SCORE website report that new business openings for 2008 were 627,200, closings were 595,600, and bankruptcies 43,546. Seven out of ten businesses last two years and fifty percent fail after five years. These numbers are extremely discouraging.

Your business can be successful and profitable. In order to have money coming in, a business needs customers. Our number one asset and number one business priority must be our customers.

If we don't have any customers, then we don't have any money coming in to pay overhead, much less a salary. Without money to pay overhead and have an income, we will eventually have to close our business and find a job. When that happens, we feel like failures. A failed business is costly financially as well as emotionally.

We need customers to have cash flow, to have an income, to stay in business, and to be successful. Without customers, our business will cease to exist. Customers are extremely important, and when someone or something is important, we make an investment of time and attention. To be successful we must invest in our customers.

To attract new customers, you are probably spending large amounts of money, time, and energy on marketing activities. Most businesses budget five to ten percent of gross receipts for marketing and advertising. The purpose of advertising is to attract new customers, assist in retaining existing customers, and build awareness of your business.

What does it cost you to attract a new customer? Hopefully you keep good business records and track where every lead comes from. If not, I highly recommend you start immediately so you'll be knowledgeable of your cost; it's different for every business.

To calculate your cost, divide the number of new customers you have had in a twelve-month period into your advertising expenditure for the same twelve-month period. My cost to attract a new customer in 2007 was $500. I had 60 new customers, and my advertising expenses were $30,000. Dividing $30,000 by 60 equals $500. Therefore, each new customer in 2007 cost me $500 in marketing dollars.

Attracting new customers through marketing is expensive. Once you have new customers, you want to retain them and keep them satisfied and loyal, because you have invested a lot of marketing dollars. Also a satisfied customer tells other people about their experience with your business.

A referral is when a new customer does business with you based on a recommendation from one of your existing customers. The cost of a referral to a business is nothing, absolutely nothing! We all need more referrals to succeed.

A referral costs nothing in advertising dollars, and neither does a repeat customer, the customer who does business with us again and again. The repeat customer returns to the same business over and over because a relationship of trust and satisfaction has been built.

Advertising is an important necessary expense, and I'm not saying you should ditch your advertising spending. The points I am making are these: Gaining new customers costs a lot of money, repeat and referral customers do not cost advertising dollars, and every single customer is important to your success.

Since customers are critical to our success and repeat and referral customers don't cost advertising dollars, we need all the repeat and referral customers we can get. The following chapters will help you cultivate repeat and referral customers through exceptional customer service and efficient, effective communication.

CHAPTER 2

The Basics of Building Customer Relationships

Customer relationships are built with clear communication, fair business practices, quality products, and exceptional service. The most important elements in building customer relationships are trust and confidence. Trust and confidence are earned through effective communication and positive actions. This is essential to a healthy, profitable business.

Customers who are truly satisfied with the job you do, plus the products and services you provide, will not take their business elsewhere. When people are totally confident in you and your business, they tell other people. Why? Because they feel good about their experience and they want to share it with others. This also proves to themselves, family, and friends their good judgment in selecting the correct business to patronize.

Communication comes in many forms. You may not realize it, but you communicate with people in more ways than just words. Yes, the words are important, but just as important are your tone of voice and your body language. You know the old saying: "It's not what you say but how you say it. It's not what you do but how you do it." Wow, it's so true.

You may know all the basic communication information and assume your employees do, too. But everyone can benefit from a review of communication information. Sometimes, we need to relearn things forgotten or things we never learned correctly in the first place.

Basic communication skills are necessary in order to connect with people, understand one another, and have good, healthy relationships. (I'll go into greater depth about communication in a future chapter.) The following information is elementary and applies not only to customers, but also to interaction with all people.

These basic guidelines are applicable to all businesses such as retail stores, service-type industries, and businesses that sell or work in the customer's home.

GUIDELINES

IN-PERSON GREETING

Let's begin at the beginning of communicating, as in a greeting.

Acknowledge people when they enter your establishment. Say "Hello, I'll be with you in a minute" or "How can I help you today?" Do not ignore them! I repeat, do not ignore them! Do not pretend you do not see them. Customers are insulted, or at the least a little peeved, when they are deliberately overlooked. Ignoring a customer sends the "you don't matter" message.

Do not judge a person by the way they're dressed, and do not assume by their appearance that they are not your customer. When you ignore a customer (and anyone who enters your store is presumed a customer), you're sending a powerful message without saying a word. You are rejecting them, not making them feel welcome in your place of business; in essence, you are telling them that they don't count.

EXAMPLE

I went into a very expensive clothing store in my hometown to do some shopping and was totally and blatantly ignored by the staff. I wondered if I was invisible. Okay, I admit I was dressed pretty poorly in cheap flip-flops and all. It became obvious the staff was ignoring me after ten minutes of the silent treatment—not even so much as a nod of the head in my direction, or any eye contact. The three clerks working spoke to the other five or six customers as they entered the store, but not one of them acknowledged me. Needless to say, I was very insulted, and I haven't returned. I told my family, "Don't bother shopping there, because they have a snobby attitude."

My experience at that particular clothing store was unpleasant. I felt unwelcomed and rejected. The effects of the employee's actions, unfortunately, will never be known to them or to the store owner. The store lost a customer and any referral customers I might have sent their way. Erroneously, they assumed I was not their customer because of how I was dressed. I am sure they thought I could not afford their merchandise, but they thought wrong.

Give everyone who walks into your business some type of positive greeting. Offer everyone acknowledgement of their presence—of their very existence. Everyone may not be your customer the minute they walk through your door, but they may be eventually, or they may tell someone about your business who then becomes your customer.

I frequent a particular coffee shop because of one special employee who is friendly and quick with a kind word. She makes me feel welcome; she seems glad to see me, and I'm happy to see her because of her attitude. By the way, I can get the very same coffee at no less than five shops in town. But I choose to spend my money at the one that makes me feel welcome. I'm a repeat customer, and repeat customers equal continued business and continued revenue.

CONNECTING

How can you make a connection with your customer? Your objective is to be friendly and put the customer at ease. By connecting with your customer you have just begun a relationship. You can make a connection in person, on the phone, or by email.

How might you connect with a customer who has just entered your store? You must be observant and ask a question or two in order to find out some little tidbit to grab onto. Then you can start a friendly conversation through which you can connect to the customer. Finding out a little something about them allows you the opportunity to relate to them through conversation. Don't ask too many questions or you'll appear nosy. Don't talk too much about yourself or you will come off as a bore. Balance is critical; ask a question or two to show interest in the other person without being intrusive. Reveal some interest or fact about yourself without boasting or boring them.

EXAMPLE

A lady called my office to inquire about a free in-home window treatment consultation. I didn't say, "Yes, I give free consultations. When do you want me to come?" Instead I said," Yes, I do offer free consultations. Did you just move into a new home?" She responded with, "We just moved here from North Carolina and I need window coverings." I remarked, "I vacationed in Asheville, North Carolina, a few years ago and loved it." In a more relaxed tone she said, "I lived just a few miles from Asheville." And thus began a short conversation about a place we were both familiar with, Asheville, North Carolina.

Do you see what happened? I made a friendly connection on the phone with the customer before we met face to face. Our connection began by me simply asking a question that started a conversation about her, where she lived before, and that I had been to Asheville and "loved it." Asheville gave us something in common, something we both could relate to, something in which to begin our relationship. That "something" could just as easily have been a dog barking, a child's voice in the background, or anything that I could inquire about to connect us.

EYE CONTACT

Making eye contact with customers shows them they have our attention and we're interested in what they're saying. When a customer is talking and we make eye contact, it demonstrates we are listening. Once eye contact is made, the customer also knows we're focused on them and nothing else. Eye contact encourages people to feel that the person with whom they are talking is honest because they can look them in the eye. Relationships are built on honesty, and eye contact says, "I am honest. You can trust me."

ATTENTION

Give the customer your undivided attention, whether on the phone or in person. Do not multitask—it isn't appropriate. Save the multitasking for home. When a customer is asking you about a product or service, make eye contact, listen to their question, and repeat the question. This demonstrates you are interested in them and what they are saying. As you repeat the question to the customer, it is clear that you understand and are listening. When you give someone your total attention, they feel as if you care about them as well as the issue or problem at hand and doing a good job. Caring or feeling an interest in another person is one of the elements to building a good relationship.

LISTENING

Listen when customers speak. We must not interrupt or talk over them even if we are sure we know what they are going to say. It's rude to interrupt someone when they're speaking. It takes patience on our part not to interrupt when we're really busy and just want to answer their question, get rid of the interruption, and go back to more important things. By listening, you are showing respect and demonstrating that you care about what they are saying. Of course, the customer may interrupt you many times. Be patient and refrain from the temptation to talk over them. Relationships are built on many elements; caring and respect are two of those elements.

CRYSTAL-CLEAR COMMUNICATION

Clear communication is essential, and it's our responsibility to communicate well. Customers do not always know the language of our profession. Do not assume your customer understands your industry's terminology or language. You may need to use visual aids and layman's terms to communicate effectively. Of course, you don't want to insult their intelligence, especially if they're familiar with the subject you're discussing. Through conversation you will be able to discern how you'll communicate, whether it is with layman's terms or industry language.

EXAMPLE

Years ago I was attempting to sell some very exquisite window coverings to an affluent male customer. As I was going on and on about swags and jabots, he looked at me and exclaimed, "I don't know what you're talking about." He clearly communicated that he didn't know window covering terminology and felt embarrassed.

It wasn't my intention to show off my knowledge or cause him embarrassment. I felt terrible, and so we were both embarrassed. From that experience I learned that everyone does not know window treatment terminology and that I needed to use drawings and pictures to relate my ideas. Lesson learned: Do not make the customer feel stupid because they don't know the terminology or language of an industry. When we've intentionally or unintentionally made someone feel stupid, they don't usually do business with us.

TRUST

Trust is confidence in the ability or intention of a person, business, or organization. Trust is a belief in the honesty and truthfulness of a person or business. To have any type of positive relationship with anyone, we need to trust each other. When a customer does not trust that we can or will do the job, they'll go elsewhere. You certainly would not do business with a person or company you did not trust or have confidence in. Chapter Four goes into further explanation about how to build trust.

RESPECT

We must show respect to our customers. Respecting them means to consider their feelings, ideas, time, and, well … them. We also want them to respect us and our business. Customers who respect us are more open to our ideas and suggestions, as well as being more pleasant to work with. Respect is another essential element for building relationships. Chapter Four goes into more detail about building respect.

EXAMPLE

This story involves two small business owners. One owns a plumbing business, and the other is a contractor. The plumber has owned his business for twenty-six years, so inexperience is no excuse for his poor behavior.

It's 2010 and the country is in a deep recession. Many business owners are in financial trouble; in fact, many have gone out of business. More than a few owners have had to lay off employees and are back to being one-person operations. So it goes without saying, every customer is important and critical to business, especially at this time.

Now, this is the situation for the plumbing business. Business is so slow the owner had to let all of his employees go and is doing all of the work himself.

A general contractor called the plumber and said, "I am working on a remodeling job, and it needs some plumbing work. Would you be interested in doing it?" Excitedly, the plumber says, "Yes, I can do the work. When do you want to meet?" They meet on the job site. The plumber looks over the job, gives the contractor a price, and they decide on a day and time the plumber is to begin work.

Plumbing work is to begin at eight a.m. Tuesday morning. The general contractor is on the job working that day and is keeping an eye out for the plumber. At around twelve o'clock the contractor calls the plumber and asks, "Where are you, man?" "Oh, something came up. I'll be there tomorrow," responds the plumber.

Tomorrow comes and the plumber finally shows up at ten-thirty in the morning. After an hour and a half of working, he goes to lunch, and he's gone for two hours. When he gets back on the job the contractor asks, "Why were you gone so long?" The plumber casually responds, "I had the wrong pipe fitting and had to go to the store after lunch." At this point the contractor is angry, and rightfully so.

Let's take a look at what the plumber did wrong in two short days.

1. Tuesday morning the plumber is scheduled to start work at eight a.m., but he doesn't show up.
2. He doesn't have the courtesy to call and inform the contractor about a schedule problem (no communication).
3. On Wednesday, the plumber shows up two-and-a-half hours late.
4. He takes a two-hour lunch break.
5. He neglects to inform the customer of his need for a parts run.
6. He never apologizes for not showing up on Tuesday or being late on Wednesday.

How did the actions of the business owner (plumber) affect his customer (contractor)?

1. On Tuesday morning the contractor was expecting the plumber, wondering where he was and what was going on. The plumber caused the contractor concern.

2. Once the contractor called the plumber and found out he wasn't coming because "something came up," his emotions changed. Now he had lost some confidence and trust in the plumber. He wondered, "Can I trust him to show up tomorrow?"

3. He had also lost some respect for the plumber (business owner) because he didn't show up for work or call about a schedule change. By not showing up or calling, he demonstrated a total disrespect for the customer, the customer's time, and the job.

4. The next day when the plumber showed up for work two-and-a-half hours late, the contractor was upset. He was disappointed in the plumber, his work ethic, and his unprofessional behavior.

5. At lunch time, the contractor assumed the plumber would be gone about an hour since he wasn't told otherwise. By not telling his customer that he would be gone longer than a normal lunch break, the plumber once again showed disregard for his customer. After lunch the contractor wondered, "Where's the plumber?" When the customer found out the plumber made a parts run, he realized the plumber wasn't prepared for the job. At this point, any trust and respect the contractor (customer) had for the plumber (business owner) had been severely damaged.

6. No positive interaction happened between these two men other than their first meeting to discuss the work to be performed.

7. Once the plumber "made the sale" and got the job, he became careless. At first glance it appears the actions of the plumber have had no effect on his business—none that he is aware of, anyway.

The actions of the business owner (plumber) will most definitely affect his plumbing business in the near and far future.

1. His customer (the contractor) has lost all trust and respect for the plumber as a businessman.
2. There will not be any repeat business from this contractor.
3. The contractor will not refer any customers to the plumber.
4. When the contractor is specifically asked about this business, he will not have good things to say, so its reputation will suffer.
5. Gross receipts are greatly impacted by repeat and referral business, so his income will suffer in the near and far future. Unfortunately, like most business owners, he will never realize that he is the problem and that he needs to change (unless he reads this book).

If you are a business owner, especially in any type of service industry such as designer, landscaper, builder, remodeler, plumber, cleaning service, and so on, customer relationships are paramount to your success. Repeat and referral business is critical for financial success. Clear, honest communication, notice of schedule changes, and trust, respect, and consideration of your customers will assist in your success.

CHAPTER 3

What Has Happened to Customer Service?

Exceptional customer service, constantly we hear about it and see wonderfully creative ads promoting it, but where is all of this exceptional customer service? It's everywhere and nowhere at the same time. Too many companies say they give great service and yet they don't—they fall short. Quite often, all we get is marketing hype, empty promises, and disappointment.

As a consumer, I'm sorry to say that I have become somewhat cynical concerning businesses keeping their promises. When a business does stand behind what they promote and do what they say they're going to do, I am surprised, thankful, and overjoyed, and I become a devoted customer.

Exceptional means out of the ordinary, extraordinary, or uncommon. Service is a helpful act; it is conduct that is useful to others, or it can be supplying someone with something. Exceptional service can be described as an out-of-the-ordinary helpful act, or as extraordinary conduct that is useful to others or supplying someone with something in an unusual way.

Why would you want to bother giving exceptional service? Because when your service is exceptional, your customers are pleased and will do business with you again and again, plus they will refer others to you. This means you don't have to constantly beat the bushes to try to find new customers.

Marketing to your repeat and referral customer is less expensive than marketing in an attempt to attain new customers. You already have a relationship built with your repeat customer; they trust you, so the sale should be easier to close, saving you time and effort. Usually, a sale to a repeat customer is larger than a sale to a new customer because they have done business with you before. They have confidence and trust in you based on their past experience. Referrals are also easier to sell because someone (usually one of your customers) has already spent the time and energy to build you up. Even though the referral has never met you, they already have a sense of trust and confidence in you. Now you need to nurture that trust and confidence. Again, selling to a referral should be easier than selling to someone who selected you from an ad or piece of marketing material.

The information given here may seem simple and so obvious that you think any idiot should know this. You're probably right. But business owners get so busy with the hundreds of decisions and daily tasks that must be done that often simple actions, correct responses, and best behaviors get overlooked. We end up taking shortcuts in service and etiquette in an attempt to save our precious time and get all tasks accomplished.

Small actions do make a difference to our customers. When I say small, I do not mean insignificant—our actions are extremely significant. You know the old adage, "actions speak louder than words." What are some things you and your employees can implement that cost nothing and can improve service to your customers? What actions can you take that will motivate your customers to do business with you again and again, plus refer others to you? Remember, repeat and referral customers mean more profit.

On the following pages are many suggestions that are easy to put into practice right now to increase your sales. You do not have to take another class, go to another conference, buy more samples, begin yet another marketing campaign, or learn a new computer program to do what I am suggesting.

The following actions will improve your customer service and therefore increase sales at no extra monetary expense. Included are a few examples of dos and don'ts. When answering the phone, have a friendly, pleasant tone in your voice. If something has just stressed you out or upset you, take a deep breath and calm down before answering the phone. The tone in your voice makes a big impression on a customer. It can say, "I'm glad you called and want to assist you" or, "I'm in a hurry and you're interrupting me."

EXAMPLE

A friend who owned a small house cleaning business learned the hard way about the impression tone of voice makes. She put an ad in the local newspaper hoping to get more business. She received a call from a potential client, but blew it with her tone of voice. When the phone rang, she hurriedly answered in a huff because she was interrupted. The caller quickly asked, "Are you the person who ran the ad offering house cleaning services?" My friend said, "Yes, do you need a house cleaner?" There was a long pause. Then the potential customer said, "Yes, but not you—not with your attitude." My friend told me that was her wake-up call. She became aware of the effect her tone of voice had. She had run an ad that had cost her time and money. The ad worked, and she received a phone call from a potential client, but her tone of voice immediately made a bad impression. Unfortunately, she never got a second chance to make a good impression with that potential customer.

Being friendly makes a big impression on people. When a customer is met with a friendly face and voice, it gives the impression that we are glad to do business with them. A smiling or pleasant face puts a customer at ease, makes them feel welcome, and emotionally encourages them to do business with us. Nobody wants to do business with a grumpy person; most of us try to avoid unfriendly people. I don't like spending my money with someone who isn't pleasant or who appears indifferent to me.

Helpfulness is another action that is powerful and only requires us to give a little of ourselves. When someone asks about a product or service you offer, show an interest and ask questions. If you don't know the answer to their question, tell them you'll get back in touch with them with the information. If for some reason you don't have the information for your customer when you said you would, call them anyway. Explain that you are still waiting for information and when you might have it. Why would you bother to call a customer when you don't have the answers? You call them because you told them you would call them on a certain day or by a certain day. They are expecting your call; they believe you will do what you said you would, when you said you would. If the customer has to get back in touch with you, then you haven't provided good customer service. In fact, you haven't given them any service.

If you own a retail store, you have many immediate opportunities to be helpful to the customer. When they enter your store, don't use the standard question "May I help you?" It is so overused, and too many customers automatically respond with, "No thanks." They don't think about what they are saying; "no thanks" just pops out of their mouth.

Try a different approach and watch their reaction. Here are a few suggestions. First, pleasantly greet them with, "Hi, beautiful day, isn't it?" Why should you waste time with a greeting? You want to acknowledge their presence and be polite and gracious because it's your store. You should treat them like a guest, and they should feel like a guest. After a minute or so, ask the customer a question such as, "What can I do for you today?" Why ask such a question? Because the customer can't answer it with a yes or no—it's a conversational question. They must answer you with a sentence, and hopefully that will lead to a conversation during which you can discover what their needs and wants are. Then you can provide them with better service.

Be understanding and patient, because it's the kind thing and the smart thing to do. Plus, it is simply good business. When people need a product or service that they know little to nothing about, it can be a challenge to understand what they're trying to convey. Your reward for being patient and understanding is usually a thankful, appreciative customer who has just made a purchase.

EXAMPLE

Once, a lady asked if I could possibly alter some of her existing custom window treatments. Naturally I showed an interest in her project and began asking some basic questions such as, "What type of window treatments do you have?" She said, "They're droolies." "Droolies" isn't a word, much less a type of window treatment. I was totally stumped about what she meant, so I asked her to describe them. She couldn't describe them for some reason, and she kept calling them, whatever they were, "droolies." At this point in our conversation, I didn't want to make her feel foolish by telling her there was no such thing as a drooly. I mustered up some more patience and continued the conversation. Eventually she made an exaggerated hand motion that gave me a clue as to what type of window treatments she might have: Swags. This customer, who did not know what type of custom window treatments she owned, spent thousands of dollars with me. It was difficult to be patient when she couldn't communicate well. And by the way, this lady was a microbiologist; she was very educated, just not about custom window treatments. By being patient and understanding, I gained a customer.

There are many other situations where we will need to exercise patience and understanding. People have bad days, get really stressed out, and at times are just plain grumpy. Their attitude usually doesn't have anything to do with us, so we shouldn't take it personally.

Return phone calls promptly! If we have a cell phone, voice mail, land line, and email address, then why can't we get back in touch with our customers in a reasonable amount of time? If we are so busy we can't return a phone call within a few hours, then we must be too busy to handle more customers.

Return all calls the same business day, if possible. When a potential customer or past customer can't make contact with you fairly quickly, they will find someone else to do business with.

EXAMPLE

Here again is another true-life example of a small business handing its customer over to its competition. The business is a heating and air conditioning company. With this type of business, emergency calls are quite frequent, because furnaces malfunction during the winter months and air conditioners go on the blink in the middle of summer. A past customer contacted the heating and a/c business with an urgent need: Their air conditioner had stopped working during a 100-degree heat wave. This was an emergency for this dentist's office; their business was affected when their patients were not comfortable. The customer called for service three times over a two-day period but got no response. On the third call, the customer left this message: "I have tried to get in touch with you for two days about my air conditioner. Since I haven't heard back, I assume you are too busy to deal with me. I have called another business to take care of the problem."

Because they did not promptly return the phone call, the heating and air conditioning business lost that long-time customer forever, and actually drove them to a competitor. When you're in a service-type business, a customer can easily become a repeat customer if they're satisfied with the service and quality they receive. They will come back again and again if they are treated well.

Honesty is the best policy, so be honest with pricing, product information, delivery times, and so on. Nobody likes to feel cheated or taken advantage of, and the truth has a way of showing up eventually.

Keep customers informed of delays. It's good customer service to inform customers of delays before a due date. This small action takes just a few minutes and demonstrates how efficient you are. It also demonstrates your desire to keep them informed. When a person is expecting something to happen or show up on a certain day, they are usually excited and anxious about it. If they aren't informed of the delay until the due date, it is a much bigger disappointment, and this does not increase their confidence in you.

Use basic polite phrases, such as please, thank you, I'm sorry, and excuse me. This is extremely elementary, but I feel it's important to touch on this subject. Use the word "please" when appropriate, such as when making a polite request. Always say "thank you" for an order your customer places. Remember—they can always do business somewhere else. "Thank you" says "I appreciate you." Saying "I'm sorry" or "I apologize" for yourself or your business is saying you regret what went wrong. "I'm sorry" isn't necessarily an admission of wrongdoing. If you are talking to a customer and someone or something interrupts you, say, "Excuse me." Using the phrase "excuse me" says "pardon me for this interruption."

When interacting with a customer, whether you are on the phone, in your store, or in their home, inform them of what you are about to do. If during a phone conversation with a customer you need to look something up, tell them, "I need to look that up, please give me a minute." Why should you bother to inform them? Because when a customer is on the phone and there is a long silence, they don't know what's going on. They wonder, "Did she cut me off, is she coming back, has she forgotten me? What's going on?"

When you're working with a customer in your store and need to look up something on the computer or go to another area of the store to find what they need, inform them. Don't just turn your back to the customer and get on the computer, or walk away to a different area of the store. The customer doesn't know what you're doing or thinking. They don't know if you're going on a break; don't want to wait on them, or what's going on. Say to them, "I need to look that up." Or, "That product is at the other end of the store. I'm going to get it for you right now." This is called courtesy, and today it is most definitely in short supply.

What if you're conducting a sales appointment in the customer's home and need to go to your vehicle to get more information or samples? Inform your customer. Say, "I need to go to the car for that sample. I'll be just a minute." Letting your customer know what you are about to do makes them feel comfortable. They are not wondering where you're going and what's going on.

Be on time for all appointments. When you're in a business where appointments are set up, either at your location or the customer's home, it is paramount to be on time. Being late shows a blatant disregard for your customer and their time. It's as if you're sending this message: You and your project are not a priority to me.

When you realize you're going to be late for an appointment, inform the customer as soon as possible. You wouldn't believe the number of business owners who arrive late for appointments and think nothing of it. Some don't bother to show up for an appointment that they themselves scheduled. If that doesn't scream "I don't care if you do business with me or not," I don't know what does.

Let your customer know how late you are going to be, and ask if you both can still meet or if rescheduling is a better option for them. By showing courtesy and respect, you have kept yourself in good standing with your customer.

Always be reliable. Customers want to do business with dependable, trustworthy people. If a customer can't depend on what you say or do, how can they do business with you? How can they possibly have confidence in you? Do what you say you're going to do, when you say you're going to do it! Customers usually hold us, business owners, to a very high standard because we are the professionals.

When in a customer's home, always show respect for them and their property. This should be common sense, but as most of us know, common sense isn't so common.

EXAMPLE

In this example, a plumber went on a service call to fix a leaky bathtub. He fixed the leak, and he knew he did a good job. Unfortunately, it was raining that day; he had mud on his boots and tracked it through the house. The customer brought the mud to his attention, but the plumber just shrugged it off.

Let's look at what happened and how everyone involved was affected. First, the plumber showed up, fixed the leak, and believed he did a good job. He assumes the customer will do repeat business with his company. However, the customer is not pleased with the actions of the plumber, even though he efficiently repaired the leak. She will never do business with him again.

Once the mud was brought to the plumber's attention, he did not apologize for tracking it in or clean it up. He didn't even bother to offer to clean it up. He showed total disregard for the customer and her property. Even though the plumber was efficient and fixed the leak, he lost a customer forever.

The customer paid the plumber and then had to go behind him and clean mud off the floors. She will always remember his attitude of indifference, and having to clean up after him.

Take time to listen to your customer. This demonstrates your ability to actually hear their concerns and needs. Of course, they don't know you are listening unless you make eye contact and verbally respond. It is rare today for a customer to actually be heard or have the feeling of being heard. When the customer realizes you are truly listening and understand their needs, wants, and concerns, they feel a sense of relief and a connection to you.

Assist the customer with information that's pertinent to their problem, need, or want. You are a professional in your field of work, so you either have a solution or can find a solution for them. Don't overload your customer with information unrelated to their situation in an attempt to impress them with your vast knowledge. Make only recommendations that will fill their needs or wants. I have found that the more talking I do, the less the customer comprehends, or the more confused they become. When I ask someone what time it is, I don't want to hear how the watch was made.

If you own a retail store and have just made a sale, there are multiple opportunities at this point for you to give exceptional service. Verbally thank the customer for their business and ask if there is anything else you can do. Offer to call them when you get in new merchandise that they might be interested in. If what they purchased is big, heavy, or cumbersome, offer to have an employee carry the item or items to their car. Tell them, "It was good to see you," and mean it. These simple gestures make a customer feel good about you and your store. When a customer feels good about doing business with you, they will do business with you again when the need or desire arises. Repeat customers are a huge asset.

EXAMPLE

This is an example of a small business giving that special touch to their customer. In my hometown is a small dry cleaner that does a great business. I don't believe it's because their prices are low or their cleaning is superior to any other dry cleaner. When a customer picks up their cleaning, the owner, a small Asian woman, comes out from around the counter and gives the customer a sincere hug and a verbal thank you. This shows the customer that they are extremely appreciated, and it makes a good impression. Since this is a pleasant and memorable experience for customers, they continue doing business with this establishment. Now, I'm not suggesting that we all hug our customers, but it works for this dry cleaner.

We must quickly solve problems that arise. We have to solve the problem sooner or later anyway, so why shouldn't we do it quickly? Many business owners put off problem solving until the customer is upset, and then they have to deal with the problem and an upset customer. Usually the business (owners and employees) is oblivious to the fact that they have added to the problem through their lack of response or interest. Do not procrastinate; it will not help you be successful. People appreciate a quick response to their problems or complaints. Problems should be a priority; they need to be solved so you can get them off your mind and move on to other more profitable tasks.

After the sale, make contact again by way of a thank-you note. Show the customer you appreciate them; send a thank-you note and possibly a thank-you gift. This can be by email, but I personally prefer a handwritten note. I've been in business twenty-eight years, and every customer receives a handwritten thank-you note with three business cards after they've received their order. I write a personalized note by hand even though my handwriting isn't pretty. It shows genuine effort on my part, which doesn't go unnoticed by the customer. Preprinted, generic thank-you cards don't show much thought or effort, so I don't recommend them.

You'll find people appreciate this small gesture. I've had customers keep their thank-you notes for years. I enclose three business cards for a couple of reasons; one for the customer to keep and the other two to be given to anyone who might need my services or products.

A phone call after the sale to make sure the customer is pleased with their purchase or service is also important. Again, it demonstrates our concern and interest for our customer. This is one of the hardest phone calls to place, and it takes real courage to place it. Why is this phone call so tough to make? We don't want to hear any negative criticism or a complaint, that's why. We business owners tend to believe no news is good news and so leave well enough alone.

More often than not you'll hear how satisfied and pleased your customers are. Many times this call sets the stage for a future sale. If by chance something is wrong, this call provides the customer, who normally wouldn't voice their complaint or disappointment, an opportunity to bring it to your attention. Many customers don't complain; they just quietly take their business elsewhere. We can't change what went wrong or apologize if we aren't aware of the problem. Gather your courage, be fearless, and make the call: Just do it.

Consistency of exceptional customer service is a critical component of business success. Give exceptional customer service every day to everyone. Make it a priority, make it a habit, and eventually it will become very natural and easy.

Losses to you as a business owner when your business provides poor customer service are as follows.

- Loss of a customer
- Loss of a sale
- Loss of profit

- Loss of a repeat customer
- Loss of referrals (potentially multiple sales)
- Loss of reputation

Exceptional service or poor service both affect the bottom line—one positively, and one negatively.

CHAPTER 4

Building Trust and Respect

Earning a customer's trust and respect takes work and effort. A person must be consistent in their professional business behavior.

Trust is confidence in the ability or intention of a person or business. Trust is a belief in the honesty and truthfulness of a person or business. Today, the general reputation of all business owners has been greatly damaged. Corrupt businesses of all types and sizes have been in the news for the past few years. Their skillful deceit, thievery, lying, and blatant disregard for others have tarnished the reputation of all business owners.

It is up to us as business owners to bring back dignity, trust, respect, and confidence to businesses once again. Consumers are skeptical, and rightfully so, considering all the deceitful business practices that have been used against them to get their money.

When a customer trusts us, they are more inclined to accept our professional advice about a product, service, or project. This usually leads to a more satisfied customer. Trust also determines whether we gain repeat and referral business; therefore, trust affects our gross receipts, our sales, and our profits.

Respect is hard to regain once it's lost, so don't do anything to lose it once you have it. Respect is having consideration for another person or idea. It's also recognizing the value of someone or something. We want our customers to respect us and our professional advice and ideas. That doesn't mean they're going to agree with everything we say or suggest. It is much easier, though, for us to get the job done if we have the respect of our customers. Of course, we must respect them, too.

Gaining and keeping a customer's respect and trust is accomplished by the positive interactions we have with them and how we complete the many responsibilities they've entrusted to us. Trust and respect build good, solid relationships.

EASY WAYS TO BUILD TRUST AND RESPECT

Dressing appropriately for the job at hand has value.

If you're a paint contractor and meeting a client to quote a job, dress appropriately. You wouldn't meet them in a suit—you would be overdressed. If you were in a suit, dressed like a banker, the client might get the impression that you charge higher prices than most paint contractors.

Potential customers have some vague idea of how a decorator like me should dress, and I'm sensitive to that. Therefore, I dress appropriately for sales appointments. I do not wear flip-flops, jeans, and a tank top on a sales appointment, because it would lessen my chance of building the customer's respect for me and their opinion of my abilities. I can't make a sale if I don't gain some measure of trust and respect.

Show up on time for appointments.

This is a simple yet powerful start to building a great relationship. Being on time shows you are responsible, can manage your time, and have respect for the customer's time. Being prompt sends a silent yet powerful message. That message is, "You and your project are important to me, and I want to do business with you."

Don't use foul language, or curse, swear, or grumble; it's off-putting.

Gossiping shows a lack of character, and it's tacky, so just don't do it. Refrain from talking about the competition, or anyone, in a negative way.

Be prepared!

Preparedness is essential to building a customer's trust and respect. Be ready for whatever it is you are doing or are about to do. If it's a consultation or an in-home sale, get your information together and be prepared; don't waste the customer's time or yours by not being prepared. Most people can tell when we aren't prepared, and this works against what we're trying to do: Gain a customer, make a sale. If you have just advertised a huge sale for a specific product, then you'd better be ready for it. Have the sale product in stock so you can sell it when the customer requests it. Don't disappoint them by being unprepared and not having the sale item on hand.

Be reliable.

Do what you say you're going to do when you say you're going to do it. This builds the customer's trust in us; otherwise, they don't know when to believe us. Live up to your commitments.

Meet deadlines or notify the customer if the deadline can't be met.

When preset deadlines can't be met, call the customer as soon as you're aware of the delay. This demonstrates your courteous, professional way of doing business and shows you care about them being informed. Most customers are appreciative of our efforts, and this builds their trust in us. When deadlines or delivery dates aren't met and the customer isn't informed and has to contact us, they begin to be disappointed, if not a little irritated, by their experience with us.

EXAMPLE

This example shows how important it is to notify customers when we aren't able to meet deadlines. I have a friend who special-ordered a couple of decorative area rugs from a local rug retailer. The retailer told him it would take about ten days for the rugs to come in. As is typical business practice today, ten days came and went with no contact from the store. My friend waited an extra ten days (now twenty days had passed) and he still hadn't heard from the store. He was anxious and excited to get his new rugs, so he called to check on his order. The store associate told him the rugs weren't in they were on back order. My friend proceeded to refresh the associate's memory about when the rugs were supposed to be in and the fact that he hadn't been notified about the back order. To my friend's surprise, the store associate asked him if he wanted to cancel his order. (Can you believe this? You and I both know this guy was not working on commission.) My friend did not cancel his order—he really wanted the rugs but he was upset about the delay and even more upset with the store associate's apathetic attitude.

What the store associate did wrong:

1. He did not notify the customer about the delay.
2. When the customer called the store, the associate did not apologize for the backorder or for not calling and informing the customer of the backorder.
3. The associate gave the impression of not caring about the customer or his order.

How did the store associate's actions make the customer feel?

1. The customer felt the business didn't do a good job of communicating and keeping him informed.
2. He was also given the impression that he was of no importance.
3. It was not a pleasant experience, and he feels he will not do business with the store again.

If you own a retail business or service-type business such as designer, landscaper, builder, remodeler, plumber, or cleaning service, ECT, trust and respect are paramount. By implementing the information in this chapter, you will be head and shoulders above your competition. If you don't put this information into practice, you are working against your success time and time again, or as I like to say, "You're shooting yourself in the foot."

A customer who trusts and respects you and your business will do business with you again and again, in addition to telling other people about you. Word of mouth is a powerful marketing tool and doesn't cost a dollar.

B

CHAPTER 5

Building an Excellent Reputation

How will building an excellent business reputation help you? The reputation of a business and its owner is what people say and think about the character and qualities of the business and owner. When people think you have good qualities and good character, they are more apt to do business with you. No one in their right mind says, "Joe the mechanic has a bad reputation. I think I'll take my car to him." Building an excellent reputation assists in gaining customers; potential customers come to us with a sense of confidence based on our reputation.

How does an owner build an excellent business reputation? It's a process that takes diligence, consistency, good decision making, effective communication, high standards, and time. It seems like an insurmountable task, but step by step and day by day we build our reputation. Why not build an excellent reputation?

Ideally, you want every task and every contact to help in building your business's reputation. Everything you and your employees do and every conversation with customers and suppliers creates an impression. These impressions build your business's reputation, either positively or negatively.

As you go about your business life, determine to do your best and be your best, because the choices you make today affect tomorrow. People who come in contact with you notice how you do things, and they make judgments; it's just a fact of life. You want their judgment of your business to be positive in order to help build an excellent reputation. As you build a great reputation, you'll gain more customers and more revenue.

Satisfied customers will help build your great reputation by telling other people about you. They will basically tell their story (testimonial) about their good experience with you. Of course, those customers who had a less than positive experience will also tell people about it, and this can work against building a great reputation.

Building an exceptional reputation is a conscious decision; it doesn't just happen. You and your employees being the best you can be and doing the best you can do at whatever business you are in is most important. Some actions and decisions, though, can work for or against a reputation, and so often they are overlooked.

These overlooked actions and decisions seem simple, obvious, or possibly unimportant in comparison to the business at hand. But believe me, to the customer these things make an impression. They help form the customer's opinion about the character, qualities, strengths, and weaknesses of you and your business.

These actions are written in basic checklist form with a brief reason for their importance. When you and your employees put them into practice, they will easily help to build an excellent reputation. A great reputation brings in new customers and assists in retaining existing customers. As you will clearly see, it is to your benefit to work toward building an excellent reputation.

- **Keep all equipment (tools, automobiles, samples, and so forth) clean and in good working order.** When tools, samples and business vehicles are in good, clean condition, this sends the message that you are attentive to detail and take pride in your business.

- **Keep all clothing and or uniforms clean, in good condition, and fitted properly.** First impressions are based on appearances whether we like it or not, so let's make a good first impression.
- **Keep your place of business orderly and clean.** Again, this shows your attention to detail and that you can control the physical workspace.
- **Owners and employees should dress appropriately for the job at hand, the type of clientele, and the geographical area in which business is being conducted.**
- **Owners and employees should be friendly to everyone.** Make everyone feel welcome with a smile and acknowledgement. We want people to feel comfortable in our establishment. We never know who the next big customer might be.
- **When using the phone, be professional.**
- **Offer respect and consideration to everyone.** It is a part of professional behavior. No one ever gained a good reputation by being disrespectful and inconsiderate.
- **Use clean language and good manners.** This shows good character.
- **Be on time for appointments.** This builds your reputation for professionalism and punctuality.
- **Meet deadlines unless the unexpected pops up**.
- **Consistency within marketing materials and throughout work performed is important to building an excellent reputation.**

Employees need clear, step-by-step instructions in order to meet our expectations. Do not assume your employees know what you want when they are given only general instructions. This is a recipe for failure, because they will interpret your instructions based on their experience and knowledge, not yours. Thorough communication is critical.

As the business owner, you are the leader; you set the standards and guidelines for whatever your business is doing. This covers everything from the business's physical condition to interaction with customers. Be consistent with your guidelines and standards; don't flip-flop back and forth.

We all know that McDonald's restaurants do not make the very best burgers, but they have great consistency in their service, cleanliness, and quality of food. When we go to any McDonalds anywhere we can count on the type of food and service we are going to receive. As consumers, when we get what we expect or better, we are satisfied.

CHAPTER 6

Keeping Customer Relationships Strong

When we keep customer relationships strong, we gain repeat and referral business. This translates into a healthier business. When we have a constant flow of repeat and referral business, we have continued business revenue.

As business revenue continues to flow in, our business stays solvent. With enough customers, business could grow if that's your intention. It is important to stay in touch with your customers after the business transactions are complete to keep strong relationships.

With all you have to do, how in the world are you going to nurture these customer relationships? Herein are multiple easy ways to nurture those relationships. You decide whether to implement all of the ideas or maybe just a few.

As you know, keeping any relationship strong takes effort and time. If you do not have the time to implement these ideas, you may want an employee to take on this responsibility.

One of the easiest ways to keep customer relationships strong is to stay in touch. This can be accomplished by a quick phone call, email, postcard, or visit. Touch base with your customers at least three to four times per year so that you and your business stay in the forefront of their minds. When you are in the back of people's minds, it's almost the same as being forgotten.

EXAMPLE

One incident stands out clearly in my mind. I had decorated an entire home for a customer, and after the job was completed I did not keep in touch with her. After thirteen or fourteen years, she called and said she needed to replace some sheer draperies. They had dry-rotted, and she needed to replace them because she was getting ready to put her house up for sale. We set up an appointment and I went to see her. During our conversation she said, "A couple of weeks ago a friend asked me if I knew of a decorator she could call, and I gave her someone else's name. I don't know why, but I didn't think of you at the time." Well, I know why she didn't think of me! I neglected to keep in touch with her, so I was in the back of her mind, not the front.

To stay in the front of our customer's mind, we must stay in contact with them; this keeps the relationship current and strong. Making a quick phone call every three or four months to your customer is a great way to stay in touch. You don't have to have a sale, give something away, or have a gimmick to call them. Simply call. Identify yourself and your business and say, "I was thinking about you and thought I would call and say hello. How are you? Is the work we did still servicing you well?" That's easy and friendly, isn't it? If you are running a promotion or introducing a new product or service, you will certainly want to tell them about it. They can't take advantage of a promotion they don't know about.

Quite often the customer will be truly happy you called because they were thinking of you and needed your services. They just hadn't gotten around to calling you. Sometimes a phone call turns into a sale; at other times, it is just a service call. Don't get discouraged if the customer has a problem with what you sold or serviced previously. Remember, the purpose of your phone call is to continue building a relationship in order to have a repeat customer for years to come. If they have a problem with something you sold them, now you have the opportunity to shine by taking care of the problem quickly and efficiently. Responding to a problem in a pleasant, efficient manner helps build a strong relationship. Who doesn't appreciate and remember a quick response? When they are ready to buy a product you offer, why would they bother with any other business when you have always taken such good care of them?

Postcards, mail, newsletters, and email are also good ways to build customer relationships. When sending this type of correspondence, make an announcement of some type such as introducing a new product or service. Announcing a sale or discount will also get their attention and keep you in their mind. Warning: Don't overdo the sale or discount promotions, or customers will come to expect lower prices all the time.

Another way to stay in touch is to visit your customer. Depending on what type of business you're in, this isn't always possible or appropriate. If you have the type of business where visits are appropriate, then go visit.

Strong relationships that supply continued business, repeat and referrals, are vital for a business to thrive.

One of my secrets to success is being committed to building a relationship with each and every customer.

CHAPTER 7

Business-to-Business Relationships

There are many kinds of business-to-business relationships. For the purpose of this book I'm going to address the one business-to-business relationship that is of most importance and also the least understood by small business owners.

I'm talking about the long-term, ongoing relationship between two businesses. This relationship may be between retailer and wholesaler, a trade-type business (a business selling their time and skill), or a manufacturer to a wholesaler or retailer. You get the idea, right?

Why is this relationship so important? A small business is not an island; it depends on other businesses, both large and small, to supply products, talent, skill, revenue, and more. In other words, businesses rely on each other.

Where I find the root of the trouble begins with the business-to-business relationship is in the understanding of which business is truly the customer and which is the supplier of goods and or skills. This may sound ridiculous, but it's absolutely true. The small business doesn't always know or understand which one of them is actually the customer.

It seems obvious: The business doing the buying, spending the money, having the demand, and so on is the customer. The business (customer) directly supplying another business with revenue knows that they are the customer. Most of the confusion is with the other business—the one supplying the service or product.

EXAMPLE

I attempted to have a business-to-business relationship with a small local drapery workroom years ago. After many months of working with the owner it became evident that she did not recognize me as her customer or place any value on our working relationship. How did I know this? Because work was never ready when the owner said it would be, she never called and gave me a status update when jobs were late, and she never apologized for being late with a drapery job. The most telling clue that she did not recognize me as her customer came when she told me she was doing me a favor.

I'm not making this up or exaggerating; she actually said she was doing me a favor by performing the work. No way was it a favor! I was paying the going rate for the work, and she dictated the pricing and delivery time, not me. I was steadily supplying work to this workroom for more than a year. Needless to say, I found another workroom and took my business elsewhere

The workroom owner didn't recognize me as her customer, placed no value on the work I continually supplied her, and had no respect for delivery dates and time frames. I'm sure she missed the income from the work I supplied her once it was gone. She did not realize her role in the relationship and that lack of professionalism caused me, her customer, to feel unappreciated. Not only that—I had absolutely no confidence that she could meet delivery dates. I had to reschedule deliveries and apologize to customers, which created extra work and embarrassment.

Over time a business may forget their position in the relationship. How can a business forget who the customer is? How is it possible for the supplier to not realize he is the supplier and not the customer? Several things happen over time that may cause a business to forget their role or position in the relationship. Because the businesses are in such close and constant contact, one or both may become lax in their approach to the relationship. One may start taking the other for granted. Over time and with familiarity, the roles of the relationship get muddled, and this causes problems.

With familiarity comes the assumption that each business knows how the other works. One business may have a basic overview of the other, but rarely an in-depth knowledge of the challenges the other faces in cash flow, employee issues, scheduling, time frames, material availability, and so on. Often we give each other too much credit for what we know about the other. We sometimes erroneously think the other business should know how we feel, what we think, and how their actions and attitudes affect us. Yeah, it sounds like a marriage thing.

So what should these businesses do? Communicate clearly and constantly with each other. Treat each other with respect. In any business, there are procedures to follow in order for the work to flow smoothly. Procedures assist in quality control, tracking production, communication, and efficiency. That being said, both businesses must know without a doubt what is expected of them. Being aware of each other's procedures, timetables, and skills will assist in developing a healthy business-to-business relationship.

When embarking on a new business-to-business relationship, which more than likely will be ongoing, it's best for both to communicate clearly from the start. Each partner in the business-to-business relationship has responsibilities to the other, and these must be clearly understood.

Each has a responsibility to follow the other's procedures as they relate to their perspective business. For example: If the supplier of your custom gizmo has a particular order form that you must complete when placing orders, then you must complete it. Why? The supplier's order form assists in his company's efficiency and prevents mistakes, and that is exactly what you want: A supplier who is efficient and makes few mistakes. We must work with each other, not against each other.

Consistency is important in any business. As the business supplier, if your turnaround time on manufacturing a gizmo is three weeks, then three weeks is what your business customer is expecting each and every time they place an order. Your customer doesn't know what to expect from you if your delivery time varies. The customer begins to lose confidence in your ability to deliver on time when delivery times vary by more than a few days. When there's a problem with meeting a deadline, contact your business customer as soon as possible and inform them of the delay. This is common sense, common courtesy, and the professional action to take. Don't be afraid to tell them the truth.

Keep in mind that this is your business customer who supplies you with constant work and revenue. You want to build and keep their confidence and trust so they continue working with you and not some other business. Remember, your business customer has a delivery schedule to meet and customers of her own to keep happy. Her customers are expecting their gizmo to be delivered at the time she told them it would be delivered. She based her delivery schedule to her customers on your delivery schedule to her.

If you're in an industry selling your time and skill, procedures still must be followed and time frames met. For instance, a business installing flooring must have procedures, measuring forms, proposal forms, and scheduling practices in order to run the business well. If the owner of the flooring installation business wants to keep his builder customers who do business on a continual basis, year after year he must be efficient, responsible, and dependable. Our customers are our most important asset. Without them we have no work, no money, and ultimately, no business.

EXAMPLE

This example is of a business performing poorly and is typical behavior of many subcontractors.

The owner of a flooring installation business is scheduled to install flooring for one of his loyal builder customers who builds twelve homes a year. Installation is scheduled to start Monday; the work will take four continuous days at a price of $4,000. Pricing and scheduling are provided by the installation business (business supplier) to the builder (business customer).

Monday afternoon the builder drops by the job site to see how the flooring installation is coming along. To his surprise, nothing has been installed and workmen are not on the job. He checks his cell phone for a message from the installer and finds none, so he calls the office of the installation business to find out what happened. The owner of the installation business says, "We got behind on a job we were working on last week. My guys will be on your job tomorrow."

Now the builder's mind is in high gear. He needs to call and reschedule several other subcontractors and deliveries because of the delay in installing. He hopes the other businesses can accommodate this sudden change in schedule. Will his project be more than one day behind schedule, and what's the delay going to cost him? Who else in town installs flooring? These are concerns and questions that run through his mind.

How did the actions of the flooring installation business (business supplier) affect the builder (business customer)? The effects are fairly obvious to us, because we've had a glimpse of the builder's thoughts and actions.

The effects on the builder (business customer) were as follows:
1. On Monday the builder was negatively surprised when he discovered the scheduled work was not being performed.
2. The builder had to waste his time calling the installation business to be informed of the situation.
3. Prearranged deliveries and subcontractor scheduling had to be reviewed and contact made to reschedule work and deliveries. What a waste of the builder's time!
4. Loss of time and productivity equals loss of money.
5. Confidence in the installation business had been shaken; the builder questioned the reliability, dedication, and professionalism of the business supplier.

The effects on the flooring installation business (business supplier) are not as obvious; in fact, it appears there are none, but they will surface eventually. Unfortunately, the installation business will never be aware of its mistakes (wrong actions) or the effects of those mistakes. If we are not aware our actions are wrong, then we cannot correct them.

The effects on the flooring installation business are as follows:

1. Damage has been done to the business-to-business relationship.
2. It has lost a portion of its reputation with its customer.
3. Loss of a business customer, which equals loss of revenue, is probable.

Remember, this builder builds about twelve homes a year.

It's a great possibility that the builder will find another business to spend his money with. He will look for a more dependable installer, or at least one who is professionally considerate enough to inform him of delays in advance.

Communication is of utmost importance. Don't make the mistake of assuming you know or understand what your business customer or business supplier is thinking, meaning, or getting at. Don't try to read between the lines—you may read the spaces incorrectly. Don't try to send subtle messages by some code, body language, or innuendo. Say what you mean and mean what you say, but always say it in a kind, professional manner. How you say something is so important. Be aware of your tone of voice, the words you use, your approach, and your timing.

Tips to Keep Your Business-to-Business Relationships in Good Shape:

- Communicate clearly.
- Confirm in writing all orders, pricing, changes, and delivery schedules.
- Respect one another's time and ability.
- Pay your supplier on time.
- Do not take advantage of one another.
- Request rush orders sparingly and expect to pay more for them.
- Have a team mindset.
- Use professional behavior and language at all times.
- Inform one another immediately if deadlines can't be met, and apologize for any inconvenience.
- When there's a problem (and there will be) discuss it calmly, fairly, clearly, and privately. Don't allow your ego or pride to get in the way.
- Remember, we are all human, we all make mistakes, and no business is perfect, just as no human being is perfect.
- Know all things are not always under your control.
- Forgive when you can.
- Apologize sincerely.
- Try you best not to lay blame on the other business, but if you must, get all the facts first. Getting the facts throws light on an otherwise dim situation.

As in any relationship, there are unwritten rules of behavior to follow. Using good common sense, which isn't very common, will benefit you and your business greatly.

CHAPTER 8

Exceeding Customer Expectations

Customer expectations, what does that mean to you as a business owner and to your customer? As a business owner, you want to (at the bare minimum) meet your customer's expectations so they will become repeat customers and refer other people to you. To the customer it means that they think, guess, feel sure of getting, or look forward to what you are offering, whether it is a service, product, or a combination of the two. You want to exceed, not barely meet, their expectations. You want to make an impression on them; you want them to be really pleased, not merely satisfied. You want them to remember you, to be in the front of their mind so they will do business with you again.

Consumers expect different levels of service, business practices, and professionalism from different types and sizes of businesses. A "one size fits all" expectation simply does not apply. For instance, a customer does not expect the backyard mechanic to offer the same speedy service or high price tag that an auto dealership's service department offers. The consumer will tolerate the backyard mechanic taking longer to do a job than expected because he is working by himself. Also, the customer is sure the backyard mechanic will not charge as much as the big dealership because he doesn't have as many expenses. The customer can accept being somewhat inconvenienced when he's sure of getting a better deal.

Do you know what your customer's expectations are? Think about it. If you really don't know, then you need to find out. You must know what they expect from you and your business in order to exceed their expectations.

So now you know what your customer's expectations are and you know you meet most of them most of the time. Is that really good enough to build a strong repeat and referral base for your business? Is that good enough to set your business apart from your competition? Is that good enough for your customer? Try exceeding the customer's expectations.

Why would you want to put a whole lot of extra effort into exceeding the customer's expectations when just plain old satisfying them is good enough, and besides, you're busy? Why would you want to make more work for yourself? You are doing the work of two people as it is, right? Selfishly, you do it to benefit yourself and your business. The customer benefits too, of course—that's evident.

Exceeding the customer's expectations benefits you through:
+ Building repeat business.
+ Building referral business.
+ Building a good reputation.
+ Improving profitability.
+ Building customer loyalty.
+ Building strong relationships.
+ Providing a sense of accomplishment and pride.

I can't tell you specifically what to do to exceed your customer's expectations because I don't know the precise business you're in. This chapter will provide you enough general information to give you ideas and help you to create ways to exceed your customer's expectations.

Exceeding a customer's expectations through the personal service and attention you give them is always a winner for everyone concerned. All of us love a little attention now and then. It makes us feel special, and who doesn't like to feel special.

EXAMPLE

In my town there is a woman's clothing store that does a great job of making customers feel special—and this is a chain store. I needed clothing for a vacation and just by chance went into this particular store a couple of years ago. I had never been there before. Now, I hate to shop for clothing. I hate trying on clothes in a little tiny changing room. And I despise having to walk out of that tiny room onto the sales floor to look at myself in a full-length mirror with price tags hanging all over me. The entire clothes shopping experience just puts me in a foul mood! Really, there are a few women in the world who don't like to shop for clothes, and I am one of them.

Anyway, there I was, and the salesperson asked if she could help me and I said yes. I explained that shopping wasn't something I enjoyed but that I really did need clothing for vacation. She was wonderful; she made the experience kind of fun. She pulled clothing from the racks and made suggestions as to what shirt would look good with a certain pair of pants. She waited for me to come out of the dressing room and offered her opinion on each piece of clothing. This salesperson gave me personal service. She made me feel special by creating a fun experience that I wasn't expecting and exceeded my expectations. Wow! Let me tell you, I spent some serious money on clothing that day.

Yes, it's easier for a clothing store to give individual customer attention than it is for many other businesses. How about a convenience store? It's not so easy to make someone feel special in a fast-paced convenience store. Most customers don't expect much from a convenience store except, well, convenience. Here are a few suggestions to exceed the expectations of the convenience store customer. Smile and acknowledge the customer when they enter the store. If you notice the customer is searching for something, ask if they have found everything they are looking for. Of course, if they can't find what they need, direct them to it. After you ring up their purchase, smile and say, "Thank you, I hope to see you again." Better yet, come up with your own sincere phrase.

Actions to exceed your customer's expectations: For one I included a brief explanation or example for clarification.

1. Be friendlier than necessary.
2. Be more helpful than required.
3. Be more polite than necessary, and always show respect.
4. Make the extra effort for the customer.
   An example of going the extra mile would be staying a little longer to help a customer with a problem, even though the store closes at five p.m. Most people would tell the customer they were closing and ask them to come back tomorrow during store hours. "Come back tomorrow" doesn't require any extra effort on our part and doesn't make the customer feel good about us or our business even though they understand.
5. Listen.
6. Show an interest.
7. Make eye contact.
8. Be on time.
9. Make a friend.
10. Take care of your customer.
11. Follow through and follow up.
12. Show appreciation for your customer.

By implementing these small yet powerful actions and paying attention to details every single day on a customer-by-customer basis, you will consistently exceed your customer's expectations. At first glance, these actions and details seem insignificant. They truly are powerful and have a cumulative effect on your business over time. You'll see your efforts pay off with repeat and referral business, as well as great customers. Additionally, these actions and details will set your business apart from your competitors.

Try to incorporate all the actions listed above over a specified period of time. For instance, set a goal to incorporate all of them within a year. Introduce one action per month. Make it a habit, and once it's routine, introduce the next action. Inform your employees about the new actions to be implemented; everyone needs to be consistent in their interaction with customers.

Educate your employees by telling them what you expect of them and why. Give them specific instructions about what to do and how to do it. Do not make the huge mistake of thinking your employees will think like you and act like you. That's not fair to them; they are not you, and they do not have the same motivation, insight, or experiences that you have.

Now, let's say you have thoroughly educated your employees about what needs to be done, how it needs to be done, and why. One more important step must be completed. Develop a simple system that you can use to confirm that the actions have been completed. The system may be as elementary as one checklist per customer completed by the employee working closely with the customer. I'm sure you can develop a workable system for your business. In small business, we owners trust our employees to be truthful and follow our instructions. We don't have the time and money to micromanage them.

PART TWO

Effective and Efficient Communication

CHAPTER 9

Listening Skills

Listening and understanding what our customer is saying are crucial to the success of our business. When we understand what the customer is talking about, we can respond appropriately.

Listening requires all of our attention. We shouldn't be multitasking when talking with a customer. Our minds can only think one thought at a time. Our minds can easily flit from one thought to the next in a fraction of a second, which make it seem as if we can multitask efficiently. In reality, we cannot think two thoughts at the very same time. Try to think two separate thoughts at the very same time. You can't do it. No one can.

Since we cannot think multiple thoughts simultaneously, we need to pay attention to the person speaking. By listening, we comprehend what our customer, employee, or supplier is saying. We need to listen to them, not just hear them talking. Hearing is a physical ability; listening is a skill.

Listening is one of the most important skills to attain. How well we listen has a huge impact on our success with customers, employees, and management, as well as all relationships.

In 1991, the U S Department of Labor Secretary's Commission of Achieving Necessary Skills (SCANS) identified five competencies and three foundation skills that are essential for entering the workforce. Listening skills were among the foundation skills SCANS identified.

If SCANS identified listening as a foundation skill for entering the workforce, imagine how critical that skill is for becoming a successful business owner.

The benefits of good listening skills are as follows:

- Understanding assignments, and instruction. Comprehending verbal instruction is critical for employees. When they don't understand their assignment or task, they become frustrated, as does management. Frustrations lead to tension, which leads to negativity, which leads to problems.
- Understanding a customer's request or problem. Requests can be met and problems solved only when we understand what is being said by truly listening.
- Building relationships with customers, coworkers, suppliers, and all people in general. People feel respected when someone listens to them. As you listen to someone, you are gaining their trust and building a relationship.
- Being aware of what the person is *not* saying.
- Showing respect and validating the value of the person speaking.
- Provides us the ability to ask thoughtful, relative questions.
- Cutting down on errors, which in turn increase profitability.

I don't believe you need an example of poor listening skills. You probably have as many examples of other people not listening to you as I do.

No doubt you have played the "telephone" game at a party where everyone stands in a line and the first person whispers a sentence in the second person's ear. The second person has to whisper what they heard to the next person, and so on. The last person in line is to tell everyone what he heard. Laughter always erupts, because whether there are eight or eighteen people playing, at the end of the game the ending sentence isn't anything like it was at the beginning. This is great fun, and entertaining at a party. In business, not listening to what is being said can cause financial and relationship problems. We business owners have enough problems to handle. Let's not make more for ourselves.

Pointers for Improving Your Listening Skills:

- Do not allow your mind to wander.
- Be physically still—do not fidget.
- Do not interrupt the speaker. Be patient and allow them to talk.
- Maintain eye contact.
- Do not multitask.
- Do not look at your watch.
- Focus on what the speaker is saying; do not get distracted by other stimuli.
- Do not answer any phones or text messages.
- Do not assume you know what they are going to say.
- Be open-minded. If you are mentally disagreeing, you can't be listening.
- Ask appropriate questions once the speaker is through talking.
- Practice listening.
- Do not allow worry, fear, or anger to get in the way of listening.
- Watch the speaker's body language as they are talking; it will help you get the gist of what they're saying.
- Pay attention to the person's facial expressions. This will help you to understand what they're attempting to convey.
- Be present where you are.

As with any skill, the more you practice, the better you become. Listening is a life skill and an active skill. Your entire life will improve when you master the ability to listen and truly understand what others are saying.

Sometimes we'll run into a person who can't seem to communicate their needs, wants, thoughts, or feelings very well. If they can't clearly express themselves, then we have to work harder to understand them. It's up to us to ask questions to get the information we need in order to help them. In essence, we play the part of a detective.

CHAPTER 10

Body Language

Reading body language goes hand in hand with listening skills. In this chapter we'll touch on the basics of body language concerning communication as it applies to work-related situations. We need to know enough about body language to assist us in understanding our customers. If you would like more information about how important body language is to communication, you can find many books written about this subject.

Body language is nonverbal communication; it's facial expressions, gestures, eye movements, body posture, and body movements. Some people have a natural ability to read body language, and others don't. Anyone can learn the basics of reading body language with a bit of knowledge and practice.

As you read body language, keep in mind it's not an exact form of language. It will help you improve communication if you take all of the individual signals of a person into account along with what's being said. Don't read one signal and assume you know what your customer is feeling or thinking. Be aware that body language varies from culture to culture, country to country.

Knowledge of body language is very helpful when working with customers, especially new customers, because a relationship has not developed with the new customer as of yet. Therefore, on this first meeting we must be alert, listening closely to what is being said as well as studying their body language. Attentiveness to how they react to what you say through their body language is helpful in how you communicate.

Most of us are good at reading body language that represents being upset or angry. We know a family member is upset when they burst through the front door in a huff, slam their belongings down with a bang, and stomp off to another room. Usually their body is tense and rigid, their jaw is set, and their face in anything but pleasant. I know you know this type of body language.

The following will give you information about how to read the more subtle language of the body. Let's begin with the head. When a person is keeping their head very still and they are focused on the person speaking, they are of a serious mind. A slow up-and-down nod of the head shows a person is in agreement or understands the information being presented. A side-to-side shaking of the head demonstrates disagreement, or possibly frustration. Tilting the head sideways can mean uncertainty, questioning, or possibly a sign of interest. When the head is turned away, the attention is diverted somewhere else. This says, "I don't want to listen or talk to you." Tilting the head back can mean several things: the person may be a visual thinker, or they may be bored or suspicious. A lowering of the head indicates a shy, timid person, or it could mean that the person has something to hide.

A furrowed brow may indicate that the listener is concentrating on what's being said, or that they disapprove. A raised brow may mean the person is surprised or very interested in what's being said. We all know these types of looks; we have seen them from our spouses, children, and parents.

When the person speaking makes eye contact, they are sending the message, "You can believe me. I am being honest." When the listener makes eye contact, she is interested in what you have to say and is attentive. If a person is frequently looking side to side, he is nervous, distracted, or lying. Excessive blinking could possibly mean he is being less than honest. Wandering eyes tell you she is probably bored. Keep in mind that some people have health issues, such as dry eyes, that cause them to blink often. You will have to figure out what is body language and what is habit or health-related based on the conversation and the multiple body signals. By alert observation you will soon be able to tell the difference between an involuntary twitch and a true body signal.

A smiling face usually means a person is happy or pleased. People who are smiling seem more open and approachable. We all love to work with a smiling, happy customer.

Hands on hips reveal a person waiting for someone or something, or possibly impatience. Let's hope you are not the one the customer is impatiently waiting for. Most likely you know some popular hand gestures from your driving experiences. I'll skip over those. A person may point an index finger for effectiveness, to make a point, or to show direction. Hands pressed together with index fingers pointed upward indicate a person is judging or making a decision. It is always a bad sign when someone's hands are drawn into fists by their sides—this person is angry and tense. You really don't want to tarry long if you notice fists.

Someone with his shoulders hunched up is tense, uncomfortable, upset, or needs the name of a good chiropractor. Crossed arms in front may mean he is opposed to what is being said or is on the defense. This action may also mean the person is closing himself off from social influences. Some people just stand with their arms crossed in front of them; if this is their normal stance, it should appear relaxed. Usually a person with crossed arms and feet wide apart is taking an authoritative stand.

People who lean forward are seeking, attracting, or possibly trying to hear what's being said. A customer seeking information might lean in, listening to the information we are offering. When a person moves backward, they are refusing or denying what's being presented.

Touching someone gently on the hand, arm, or shoulder is a form of communication. This action shows encouragement, concern, sympathy, friendship, or caution. Often during a sales presentation I will lightly touch a customer on the arm as a form of encouragement and friendship. I only touch someone if I feel this will be beneficial to them, to help put them at ease with their decision and with me.

When someone props up their head with their hand, they could be tired or bored. Some people will do this when they're thinking or evaluating what was just said. Of course, this action could be habit and nothing more. Look for other signals to figure out if you are boring them.

At times someone will mirror or copy the person they are talking with in an attempt either consciously or unconsciously to put the other person at ease or to establish rapport. How that works is when someone leans back in his chair and crosses his legs the other person mirrors or copies him, leaning back in their chair and crossing their legs.

Often a person's body language communicates their attitude or intent. Then again, some gestures are nothing more than habit or a chance movement. As I mentioned earlier, observe all a person's body language, along with the conversation. Do not take one gesture, read it, and think you know what is going on in the other person's head. Reading body language is another tool to help you to understand and communicate with customers and employees more efficiently and effectively. As your communication and comprehension skills improve, so does your business life. When there are fewer errors in communication, business runs smoother. Through comprehension we have the ability to understand and the skills in which to do so.

Chapter 11

Reacting and Responding to Customers

How do you and your employees react and respond to your customers? Do you know how your reactions influence the customer's opinion of you and your business? What kind of message is your response or lack of response giving to your customer?

As often is the case with businesses, we say one thing and do another. This chapter will make you aware of any negative signals you might be sending to your customers through your reactions and responses. The messages and signals you send should be the right ones, the signals you think you're sending.

How do you and your staff respond to your customer's requests, complaints, or suggestions? Your responses may depend on whether you are reacting to a request or complaint. Many times how we respond depends on what type of customer we are working with and whether they are old, young, timid, demanding, angry, or pleasant.

Under normal working conditions, we respond pleasantly and quickly to a request from a sweet, smiling customer. When the request is for something routine and it takes normal effort on our part, we are pleasant, friendly, and helpful, and the customer is pleased.

What if the customer is impatient, in a foul mood, or has a complaint? We must be careful not to react to the customer in a negative way. A negative response will only make matters worse for all involved. The customer will get defensive and probably more unpleasant. Our response should be one of patience, understanding, and concern. Depending on the customer's attitude, this can take a great deal of self-discipline and self-awareness on our end.

Below are ways in which business owners and employees react and respond to customer suggestions, requests, and complaints. Many of our reactions and responses work directly against the success we're trying so hard to achieve. This information will bring to light the unspoken messages your reactions and responses may be sending to your customer.

LIP SERVICE

Do you ever give customers lip service just to get them off your back? A lot of businesses today have made lip service a habit. I sincerely hope you have not fallen into the bad habit of telling a customer you will do something for them when you know you won't. The minute the customer is out of sight, off the phone, or off line, you totally forget about them.

How does giving lip service—basically lying—affect customers and their opinion of us? At first when we tell a customer we are personally going to check on something or find something out for them, they are happy with us. They think we're helpful, caring, and service minded. They think they have come to the right place. After a period of time of not hearing from us—usually a few days—the customer wonders if we will ever contact them. They may now realize we were just giving them lip service. At this point, the customer feels let down by us and disappointed that they do not have an answer to their request. Now they must decide either to contact us again or to go somewhere else for an answer to their situation. We may get lucky—they may give us another chance. Usually the customer just quietly goes away and finds another business that will take care of them.

SLOW RESPONSE

Our response time makes an impression on our customers. When they contact us with a question or request, normally they expect a response that same day or, at the latest, the next day. Responding quickly to the customer builds their confidence in us and reinforces their good decision to do business with us. Contact the customer immediately even if you don't have an answer to their request and inform them that you'll get back to them as soon as possible with an answer. Too many businesses let too many days or weeks go by before returning calls, texts, and emails.

Some owners and employees take the attitude of, "When I have the answer, I will contact the customer." But it may take days or longer to get the answer; worse yet, you might even forget about them. It's rude and unprofessional not to respond quickly to a customer.

What's the effect on our customer and their attitude about our business when we don't respond promptly? They begin to try to figure out what's going on. They begin to wonder if we are too busy to get back with them, or if their request is so small we don't want to bother with it. Did we forget about them, or should they contact us again? They may also be searching for another business to work with.

We are an impatient society. As customers, we want what we want when we want it. We view quick response times as a form of good service. Therefore, slow response times equal poor service. When we respond slowly to customers, they begin to question if it's a good idea to do business with us. Responding to customers within twenty-four hours is the first step in building their confidence.

AGREEMENT AT ALL COSTS

Customers search out a professional for their expertise when they need a product or service. They are looking for a business with a knowledgeable owner and skillful employees. Most customers want the advice of an expert even though they may have strong opinions of their own. Some customers proudly announce they have done "their research."

When a customer has a strong opinion about what she wants and you know you have a much better solution or product, do you present it to her? I hope you do offer the better solution. Whether she accepts it or not is, of course, her decision. It requires time and effort to explain a better product or better solution to customers. It takes educating them so they can understand your expert advice. Some customers are so opinionated and overbearing that we may be tempted to agree with whatever bad idea they have. Don't do it.

Remember, you are the professional, and if you agree with the customer's bad idea just because it's the easy thing to do at the time, it will come back to you. I am speaking from experience! Every time I agree with an overbearing or misguided customer because I am too tired or lazy to explain a better solution or product, it comes back to haunt me. I end up paying for my mistake one way or another, because in the end, they aren't happy. An unhappy customer does not turn into a repeat customer or refer other people to us.

INDIFFERENCE

Do you show concern and interest for your customer and their purchase? I hope so, because if you do not, you are demonstrating indifference. If our customer senses that we don't care about them and their purchase, it becomes impossible for us to gain repeat and referral business.

Customers are expecting and hoping that we will take an interest in them as well as meet their needs. Showing interest is as simple as asking relevant questions, making eye contact, giving them our undivided attention, and listening. Offering valuable, professional advice that demonstrates our desire to do a great job for them is the opposite of indifference and is what we should do.

We seasoned business owners know we can't please all the customers all the time. There will always be that person who complains no matter what we say or do. Just be thankful that person isn't in your life on a permanent basis. One more thing: Don't spend too much time beating yourself up over a customer you couldn't please, especially if you know you did your best.

EXAMPLE

In my second year in business I had a very difficult customer, or as I like to say, a hyper-reactive customer. This customer had purchased wallpaper and window coverings in a companion fabric. She called to complain about the wallpaper and fabric not matching exactly. As luck would have it, she called late the day before I was to leave on a family vacation. I was thirty-three at the time, and this was my first real family vacation—we were going to Disneyland. I showed concern for her complaint on the phone by asking questions and discussing the issue in depth. What I discovered was that the paper and fabrics were exactly what I had shown her and what she ordered. Once everything was installed, she thought the paper and fabric should match exactly. However, they were never intended to match exactly—they were companions. I explained this to her and told her I would contact the wallpaper company and discuss the issue when I returned from vacation. (This was twenty-five years ago, before you could do business from anywhere with cell phones and email.) She became very angry and threatened to lodge a complaint with the Better Business Bureau. In a very loud voice she also told me I was more interested in my vacation than her and her problem, and then she hung up. After her outburst I could see I had not conveyed to her the depth of my concern. She thought I didn't care about her and her complaint.

To say this customer put a damper on my vacation is an enormous understatement. The entire week of vacation I questioned my ability to be a good business owner and seriously thought about closing my business. The first day back to work I called my wallpaper sales representative to discuss my customer's complaint. The salesman informed me that my customer had indeed called the company to complain and that he had spoken with her and taken care of her complaint. In a very authoritative voice he said, "I told her it wasn't supposed to match." Wow, he was the expert; he had gotten through to her when I couldn't

I learned a few things from that experience. One is that the customer is not always right. Don't let one difficult experience paralyze you and crush your dream of being a business owner. There are hyper-reactive people who love drama, who love to upset everyone and anyone they can, and who can never ever be pleased by anyone or anything. Also, never ever tell a customer when you are going on vacation. Just say, "I will be out of town."

Chapter 12

Lost Opportunities

Have you lost out on opportunities to do business with someone? You may not think so, but you and your employees have probably lost out many times and not realized it.

Some ways that small business owners miss out on opportunities are easy to understand. A small business may not be able to handle a large order in a timely fashion; therefore, the customer must take their business elsewhere. At times the business owner may not have the product, skill, or knowledge to do the job and must refuse it. If this is the case, I recommend you look into getting the skill or knowledge needed. Of course you'll want to research the cost and time involved in attaining skills and knowledge before making a commitment.

What about missed opportunities that aren't so obvious? We have all heard the old saying, "I wasn't in the right place at the right time." That may be true; at times we miss an opportunity due to timing

A missed phone call or an overlooked email can also be a missed opportunity. A potential customer contacts you by phone, email, or in person when they have a need or want. If you miss the call or overlook the email, you may have missed an opportunity to do business. If you're like me, you need every single sale and every single customer to survive in business today.

During the spring of 2009 my business was in a transition. What I didn't know until later was that I had lost several opportunities to do business with new customers during that time. In the fall of 2009 while I was at a social function, I introduced myself to a young woman. As the conversation went on she said, "I called your business in the spring several times to get an appointment and no one ever called me back, so I called someone else." I was very embarrassed and apologized sincerely. If this woman had not spoken up and informed me of what happened, I would never have known. Often we are never aware of how or why we have lost business opportunities. If we aren't aware of what needs improvement, we can't improve on it.

What about the social function you attended when you didn't feel like meeting new people so you stayed to yourself? You were there in body but not in spirit. You might have met someone at that function who needs what you provide, but they weren't aware of you and your business. People like to do business with people they know; it gives them a sense of security.

I met a new friend, a young man, at a Chamber of Commerce mixer not long ago. Since then we always speak and talk for a few minutes when we see each other. He called me not long after we met because he was in need of window treatments for a home he had just purchased. He said, "I need blinds and curtains and you were who I thought of." I was thrilled; he remembered not just me but what my business offered. The Chamber of Commerce mixer produced a client for me not because I am a member but because I am a member who shows up and introduces herself to others.

Opportunities may also be missed as the result of lack of communication. I have lost many opportunities with existing customers because I neglected to fully communicate all of my product and service offerings. You're probably wondering how that could be. I sell many custom products and don't always take the extra time to explain my full line of products to the customer. I get upset with myself when a customer says, "I didn't know you sold blinds. I just bought blinds from someone else." Communicate to everyone you meet all of the products and services you offer. You never know who is going to need what you supply. You might meet someone today who wants what your business provides.

Slow response time can cause missed opportunities. Recently I heard of a small local plumbing business that is struggling to survive, yet the owner missed (gave away) opportunities presented to him. In one day he received three calls requesting service. He should have jumped on those calls, because business is slim, he needs money, and he needs more customers to survive. Surprisingly, though, he did not respond to those calls immediately. He wasn't in the office, so the bookkeeper answered the phone and told the potential customers the owner would call them back as soon as possible. When the owner came into the office, he was given all three messages. You would think he would have been elated to have potential customers and called them that very minute, but he did not. He fiddled at his desk, worked on an estimate, and did second things first — not first things first. Finally, late in the afternoon, he returned those three phone calls. He set up one service call. The other two potential customers called his competitors (other companies) because they needed service and had not heard back from him

There was absolutely no reason, good or bad, for the plumbing business not to have scheduled three service calls. The customers had an urgent need; the plumber had an urgent need for more business and money. Why were the opportunities lost? They were lost because the business owner did not respond quickly to the needs of the potential customer. They were lost because of mismanaged time and resources. As I like to say, "The owner shot himself in the foot."

If you as the owner or manager truly have too many responsibilities, then delegate. Select someone on your staff and give them the responsibility of contacting customers, setting up appointments, returning calls and emails, and so forth. Be sure to communicate to your employee that this responsibility is a high priority. You may be under the misconception that you are the only one who can do the job correctly. Don't kid yourself; if you are taking too long to respond, then the job isn't getting done correctly. Opportunities for business are missed, and missed opportunities equal missed revenues.

Our actions and attitudes can also be the cause of missed opportunities. How can that be? Take a hard look at your actions and attitudes. Then ask yourself if they are what you want your customers to see. Are you and your employees' actions and attitudes an accurate representation of your business?

Do your employees hang out at the front door of your business smoking cigarettes? If they do you need to change where your employees smoke. An employee hanging out at the store's front entrance smoking makes a poor impression to customers.

If your employees have a habit of gossiping or complaining when customers are present, this must stop. A customer may not want to listen to the conversation between employees, but often they can't help but hear it. Complaining and gossiping have many negative effects. For instance, when a customer hears an employee complaining about her unfair boss and how much of a jerk he is, this makes a negative impression. When the customer gets a bad impression or feeling about the boss, whether the information heard is true or not, they may decide to take their business elsewhere.

Foul language makes a very bad impression and has no place at work. No one should be cussing on the job; it is offensive and unprofessional. Make absolutely sure all employees know you will not tolerate foul language. If you're an actor, then cussing and R-rated movies sell tickets. Everyone else must refrain, because it works against our success.

Usually customers can pick up on a person's attitude. Attitude is a way of thinking, feeling, or acting, and it does show. An employee with an obvious "I don't want to be here" or "I don't care attitude" can cause lost opportunities. Nobody likes doing business with someone who doesn't care or doesn't want to work. Remember: Customers have a choice as to where they spend their money and whom they spend it with.

Poor personal appearance and hygiene is another reason business opportunities can be lost. Entire books have been written on how to dress for success. I am not going to tell you how to dress or what color shirt to wear with what color trousers. It is important to make a good first impression, second impression, and so on with every customer. All employees and owners need to wear clean, neat, appropriately fitting clothing.

Everyone we employ should have clean hair, clean bodies, and clean clothing. Their fingernails should not have dirt under them unless the type of work performed, such as mechanical work, prevents them from keeping their fingernails clean. You wouldn't want the doctor performing surgery on you to have dirt under her nails.

Body odor and stale cigarette odor are very offensive, as is trying to cover it up by spraying oneself with air freshener. This combination of smells is sickening to everyone but the person wearing them. I know a local (not so successful) business owner who always stinks and always looks like a slob. Of course he's not aware of his offensive odor or appearance. He smells of garbage, cigarette smoke, and cheap air freshener—yuck. Why he smelled of cigarette smoke and air freshener was obvious to me. It took a little longer to figure out the garbage smell. He eats a lot of fast food and keeps all of the bags, wrappers, and trash in his truck. The back seat, front passenger seat, and floor of the truck are covered with trash from fast-food restaurants. Stench is a real turn-off to everyone. Make a good impression by having good hygiene.

Appearances are also important. A person should dress the part or dress appropriately for the position they hold. The clothing of all employees and owners should be clean, unwrinkled, and fit correctly. When people are busy and have too many obligations, this can be difficult to do on a daily basis, but it should be a priority.

Dressing appropriately should be apparent. When in doubt, check out how other successful people dress who hold positions similar to yours. If you had an appointment to see a lawyer and he was sitting behind his desk in sweat pants, a ratty old T-shirt, flip-flops, and a three-day growth of beard, you would probably be stunned. I doubt you would be impressed in a good way. You might ask yourself if you should take this guy seriously. How good a lawyer can he be if this is how he's dressed? It's doubtful you would do business with him.

When you meet a representative, an employee, or an owner of a company you're considering doing business with, are you going to make judgments? Darn right—you would be foolish not to. You're about to spend your money, so you are going to judge them. You are considering trusting them enough to do business with them.

When you meet someone for the first time, how do you size them up (judge them)? Most of us use several senses to make a judgment about whether to trust someone enough to do business with them. One of the many senses we use when meeting someone for the first time is our sense of sight. How do they look? Are they neat or sloppy, clean or dirty? Is their fashion style conservative or modern? We gather this information in seconds to help us in our decision making.

Also, through our sight we observe the person's behavior. We watch their facial expressions and body language as we size them up. Do they seem as if they would be pleasant to work with? Do they appear patient or demanding?

We pay attention to the person's voice, too. Usually, we're very aware of their tone of voice as well as what they're saying. Therefore, we are using our sense of hearing to help us judge whether we want to spend our money with them. Is their tone of voice calm or frantic? Do they speak clearly, slowly, or quickly? Do they speak definitively or vaguely?

Our senses help us decide if we want to do business with a particular person or company. We use the information we see and hear to assist us in making judgments. Your potential customers use the same senses to make judgments about whether to do business with you.

You and your employees represent the business. The average customer equates owners, managers, and all employees with the business. They don't separate the individual person from the business during working hours, unless they know them personally, outside of work. That being said, everyone must look the part, be neat and clean, use good manners and appropriate language, and be the best they can be at all times. You don't want any lost opportunities!

Of course, if you want to make it hard on yourself, do what you want to do and dress whatever way you want (rock stars are excluded—they can do whatever they want and still make a ton of money). To gain a potential customer's confidence, be prepared to work harder to be taken seriously. Will you grab an opportunity or lose an opportunity to do business with someone today?

A friend of mine, a small business owner, hired her teenage granddaughter to work part time during the summer. When she hired her granddaughter she told her no BB&B allowed on the job. Her granddaughter asked her what she meant. Grandmother said, "No butts, bellies, or boobs are to show at work." Now, that's really good advice for all employees unless, of course, you're the owner of a strip club.

Chapter 13

Consistency from Marketing Through the Sale and Beyond

What is marketing? It's business communication, presentations, advertising, promotions, public relations, websites, brochures, and so on.

Marketing is everything a business puts in front of the public. It is how a business communicates to the world. Marketing is how we introduce our business, products, and services to our potential customers. It's also how we stay in front of and keep in touch with our existing and potential customers.

Being consistent is vital for business success. What a consistent business promotes in marketing, it should also do in practice. Marketing messages, whatever they may be, should align with the actions of the business.

EXAMPLE

A local appliance store promotes next-day delivery on any item they have in stock within a twenty-mile radius, Monday through Friday, excluding holidays. This service is marketed very well in all of their written advertising, websites, and other materials. The local residents have read and listened to this message over and over for years. When local residents shop at this appliance store, they are sure their new appliance will be delivered the next day. The marketing has been consistent in promoting next-day delivery.

The customer believes the appliance store's message about next-day delivery service. In order for there to be consistency from marketing through the sale and beyond, the store must offer and be able to deliver the appliance the day after it is purchased. This is consistency from the marketing message through the sales process and finally to the service given.

In order for there to be consistency from the marketing message through the sale and delivery, communication must take place. Whoever decides what the marketing messages are must clearly communicate this information to all employees. Employees need to know what the marketing messages are, how to carry them out, and what exclusions there are, if any. They need to know the specifics.

If an employee of the previously mentioned appliance store was not aware of the next-day delivery policy and a customer had to bring it to their attention, the employee appears uninformed. The customer may feel the employee is incompetent or may assume management is to blame for not training their employees; any number of negative thoughts may run through their mind.

You probably have spent and continue to spend a small fortune on marketing. I'm sure you are well aware that planning and executing a marketing campaign is fairly easy, but very expensive. When the marketing campaign is successful, it drives potential customers to your business.

Once the potential customer contacts your business, the real work begins. Taking care of the customer, meeting their expectations, and living up to the marketing message is important.

Every one of your employees must be informed about the marketing campaign. Employees must be trained as to what is expected of them, the process they are to follow, and company policies. Employees are not you—they can't read your mind, know what you know, or be expected to just figure it out. It is your responsibility to make sure they are informed and trained to your satisfaction. Your employees must know what to do and how to do it so all customers are satisfied customers

One gripe I hear all the time concerning companies is their lack of personal phone assistance. We're all so sick of phone menus and phone trees that we could scream, and some customers have. When I call a company with a question that doesn't fit neatly into their miniscule list of menu questions, I am infuriated that I have to listen to all their crap until I get a real person, if that's even possible. Don't these companies know that most customers are angry by the time they're allowed to talk to a real person?

If you are reading this and you happen to own or are in charge of a large company, then **put people to work. Hire *real* people to answer your phones.**

Another huge complaint is this standard response to a customer's question: "You can find that on our website." That response angers and frustrates most people. "You can find that on our website" is *not* customer service! I call a company for service, for an answer, for assistance, to talk to a real live person. The last thing I want is someone dismissing me quickly by telling me to go to their website. If I wanted to go to their website, I would have done so.

Not everyone owns a computer or wants one. Not everyone wants to order online, look it up himself, or do it himself. Some people still want assistance from a human being. Telling a customer to go on your website to find what they want or to place an order is like telling her to go take a hike.

Of course, there are ways to gently direct customers to your website so they can place their order or find the information themselves. We can offer an incentive such as a discount if they go online and order. If the customer has questions, though, it would be in our best interest to answer their questions and then invite them to visit the website.

Have you ever had a marketing campaign flop? Take a closer look at the possible reasons why. Maybe the marketing message was perfect, but that is where it ended—with the message. Could it be there wasn't any follow-through from the message into the sale and through the service? Could your marketing campaign have flopped due to poor consistency? Possibly the business actions were not in keeping with the marketing message. When you discover the truth about why your marketing campaign wasn't as successful as you hoped, then you can correct what went wrong and where it went wrong.

Several positive things happen when there is consistency: Customers are pleased, their faith and confidence in your business has increased, and therefore you are confident and successful. Your repeat and referral business will increase in time because of happy customers, and that means more revenue.

As consumers, we hear businesses touting how great they are, how low their prices are, what quality products they have, and on and on. We have become skeptical of these promises. But being human, we want to believe the marketing messages; we hope the truth is being told and that the business is not exaggerating or putting a spin on the information. Honesty, consistency, and integrity from the marketing message on through the sale and beyond are vital to the success, longevity, and reputation of any small business.

Chapter 14

Communication and Behavior in the Customer's Home

Selling, consulting, or working in the customer's home versus a store or office requires different behavior. When we're in our store or office, we are comfortable, we know where everything is physically, and we have all of our tools and supplies at hand. When working in the customer's home, we're in an unfamiliar environment, and that requires us to work differently than in our office or store. It requires more effort on our part.

Who works in the customer's home? Some sales people such as designers, decorators, landscapers, and insurance representatives sell in the home. The service industry in the United States is huge, and a tremendous amount of service-type work is done in the home, such as appliance repair, carpet installation, home improvement, and cleaning services. How a company representative communicates and behaves in the home will have either a positive or negative impact on the customer and therefore the business.

Remember, the goal of the salesperson is to make a sale. Therefore, they should make a positive impression on the homeowner. People don't buy from people they don't like or from someone who makes a negative impression. People buy from people they like, trust, and respect.

Every little thing you do creates either a good or bad impression on the customer. How should a salesperson act, whether they are the owner or top employee, in the customer's home? First, be on time for your scheduled appointment. This demonstrates your respect for the customer's time and the importance of the appointment. Make sure the vehicle is clean, at least on the outside, because customers notice and a clean vehicle shows you take care of things. As you approach the door to the home, stand up straight and walk briskly. Even if you don't feel it, pretend to have a little life in you. Nobody wants to buy from someone who acts like they're half dead, sick, or doesn't care about the appointment. Knock on the door, then step back a little or turn slightly so when the customer opens the door you aren't right in their face.

Once the customer opens the door, smile, introduce yourself and your company, and then give them a business card if this is the first time you have met face to face. I once sold a job to a lady, and when I got ready to leave her home she asked me what my name was. I had neglected to introduce myself or give her a business card. If you've been to the home before, start with a big smile and a "good to see you again," or something to that effect. Do not step over the threshold into their home until they invite you in.

Now that you're in the home, how do you communicate and behave in order to gain their trust and respect and create an all-around positive impression?

Take a few minutes to put the homeowner at ease. Compliment the home or something in it, and always be sincere. Try to make a connection with the customer. If you notice a motorcycle in their driveway and you also have a motorcycle, strike up a conversation about riding. Whatever conversation you start should focus mostly on the customer. Do not focus on or go on and on about yourself. This time is all about the customer—not you.

Once you've put the homeowner at ease and they think you're a pretty decent person, it's time to go to work selling whatever it is you sell. For you to present information to the homeowner, you both must sit somewhere. Ask, "Where would you like to sit so we can discuss your project and I can show you some ideas?" When they say the kitchen, you follow them into the kitchen. You see, during this entire time from the opening of the door until you both sit down to discuss their project they are leading and you are following. They've been treating you as they would a guest, because in a way you are. They made the appointment and they invited you into their home. In return, you are to behave like a guest. Be on your best behavior, and respect them and their belongings. If you need something, ask.

We want the customer to be comfortable, and most people are comfortable in their own homes, especially when they feel in control. In this pleasant, friendly atmosphere you can present whatever it is you're selling or offering in a relaxed, easy manner. Watch the customer's body language and tone of voice for direction with your presentation. For example, if the customer is getting fidgety, it may be a clue that your presentation is taking too long and they're getting bored.

Act like a guest on your best behavior. If you need to use the bathroom, ask. If you need to go to your car to get something, inform them of what you're doing and make sure the door is unlocked so you can get back in without having to ring the bell. Do not pick up, open, or touch anything that belongs to the homeowner without asking. A wallpaper hanger was working in my home once, and he wanted some salt for his lunch but did not ask. Much to my surprise, he opened my kitchen cabinets, hunted for, and found the salt. If he had asked me for salt, I would have gladly given it to him. By opening my kitchen cabinets, he overstepped his boundaries and made a poor impression. I have never had him back to work for me or any of my customers.

When selling window treatments I need to measure the windows, and sometimes a customer's furniture is in the way. Out of respect for the customer and their things, I always ask, "May I move your chair, because I need to measure your windows?" Often the customer will assist me in moving a piece of furniture, or if the piece is small they'll move it themselves. The main lesson here is to ask the homeowner if it's okay to do something *before* you do it. Always be respectful of them and their possessions.

After making the sale, inform them of how their project will progress. This is a new experience for them, and they are looking to you for information and guidance—you're the expert. They need to know how and when work will be performed, general delivery dates, completion dates, time frames, guarantees, and payment schedules.

It's critical to communicate important information to customers both verbally and in written contract form. As you relay information verbally, the customer can ask questions and get most answers immediately. When people know what to expect, they are more at ease. Informed customers are usually easier to work with, and that makes our job more pleasant. People like to be informed of what's going to happen and when, especially since they're paying for it.

Thank them for their business, make eye contact when you thank them, and be sincere. If it weren't for them doing business with you, you might be out of work.When we do a good job of communicating all information to the customer, it is easier for everyone concerned. When a job goes smoothly, you eventually gain more business through repeat and referrals

What about the repairman, carpenter, electrician, wallpaper hanger, painter, and so on? How should they behave and communicate in the customer's home?

Basic Rules of Conduct

- Be on time. Call if you're going to be more than ten minutes late.
- Have a clean appearance. Wear shoe covers in the house.
- Introduce yourself by name, the company you represent, and the reason for your visit.
- Ask the homeowner to show you where the _____ is that you are to service. Do not wander through the customer's home.
- Be neat and clean with your work. Leave the area around where you are working as you found it. (Don't make a mess for the homeowner to clean up.)
- If you need to use the bathroom ... ask.
- If you need to turn off the electricity or anything else, inform the customer that you need to turn the _____ off. Inform them before you turn something off; it's just common courtesy.
- If the item cannot be repaired at this time for whatever reason, tell them and offer options to their problem.
- Once you have completed the job, check your work. Does the item run/work? Does the work area look like you found it, or is there a mess to clean up?
- Inform the customer that you have repaired the item, and give them a brief description of what caused the problem and what you did to repair it.
- Present a bill that states the work performed and parts supplied for them to sign. Get payment if that's your company's policy.
- Thank them for their business.

If by chance you and the homeowner are talking and getting to know each other a bit, that's great, but don't bring up any controversial subjects. Don't let any of your prejudices show, don't talk about your problems, and don't talk much about yourself. Don't use foul language and don't talk poorly about your competition.

Remember as you stand in front of the customer that you represent the business. Everything you do and say is a reflection of the business. Use common courtesy and manners at all times.

Chapter 15

Reasoning Skills

One of the most crucial skills a successful business owner needs is the skill to reason or the ability to think things through logically. You can find in-depth information on the Internet to improve your reasoning and critical thinking skills. The purpose of this chapter is to make you aware of reasoning skills and what influences reasoning in the hope that you will review how you reason things out or how you draw conclusions. As you become aware of how you draw conclusions, you can improve on your reasoning and therefore improve your decision-making and problem-solving skills.

When we are reasoning in order to make a decision, we are listing choices, identifying potential problems, prioritizing, and identifying potential consequences in our mind. You may be surprised by all this mental activity taking place in your mind before you make a decision. The next time you have an important decision to make, be aware of your thought process.

We all want and need to make smart business decisions and correct problems when necessary. Good reasoning skills help us do just that.

To improve your reasoning:

1. Get the facts.
2. Raise important questions and gather information.
3. Be aware of how your emotions influence your thinking and your decisions.
4. Be mindful of how your decision will affect others.
5. Actively evaluate the information you have compiled through observation, experience, reflection, and communication.
6. Weigh the options.
7. Estimate the negative or positive consequences.

Many factors influence how we make decisions, and we usually aren't aware of all of them. Social status, culture, age, experience, religious beliefs, education, knowledge, psychological health, and ethics are many influencing factors.

To improve your reasoning skills, evaluate your thinking.

Questions to ask Yourself to Help Evaluate Your Thinking

- Am I focusing on my own reward?
- Am I trying to control something that I don't need to control?
- What are my feelings right now?
- Am I angry, afraid, tired, or frustrated?
- What is fair for all concerned?
- Do I have all the information I need to make a decision?
- Is the information accurate and relevant?
- Am I being logical?
- Have I interpreted the information correctly?
- Am I assuming something I shouldn't?
- Have I weighed all the options?

Delay decision making temporarily if you are overly tired, upset, angry, sick or hungry. These feelings can negatively influence our decisions.

Chapter 16

Email, Mobile Technology and Social Networking

Most of us use email many times a day from our multitude of devices. Now I wonder how I ever conducted business efficiently without it. Email is fast, easy and low cost to no cost.

In addition to using email for quick contact with customers and suppliers, email newsletters are a great way to keep in touch. You might also consider an email campaign to your customer list on a regular basis such as once a month or once a quarter. Of course once you start a newsletter you will need to stay on schedule with it because people will be expecting its arrival.

Email newsletters and campaigns are monetarily inexpensive but do consume time and energy. As a new business owner you probably have more time and energy than money to commit to this endeavor. In the future when your time and energy are at a premium you might consider hiring someone to take over a portion of those duties.

Campaigns

If you are sending announcements of services offered and new products to potential customers, space the email notices over time, maybe one a week. One of my suppliers drives me crazy because I will not hear from him for 3 weeks or more and then I get 4 to 6 email announcements, one after the other on the same day. Often I don't bother to open them because it's so annoying.

There are a few guidelines to follow when using email to communicate with business contacts and customers.

1. You are a professional so don't sound too casual in content.
2. Respond to emails within 48 hours.
3. Avoid slang, emoticons, jargon, and so on.
4. Don't respond when you're angry because you may regret it.
5. Keep public and private email separate.
6. Do not hit "reply all" unless all need to know.
7. Subject line should align with message.
8. Make email clean and easy to read not cluttered.
9. Briefly introduce yourself, don't assume the person knows you unless you have had recent contact with them.
10. Don't overuse the high priority option.
11. Make email short and to the point but not curt.
12. Always include a signature.
13. Reread before sending.
14. Be careful with humor: it's hard to "get" humor when we can't hear the person's voice or see their facial expressions.
15. Your email address should include your name or your company's name.

Customers are Important

I have advertised in my local newspaper regularly for more than 30 years. I write my own ads so all the paper has to do is the layout. Every couple of years the paper has a new ad representative and usually they contact me to introduce themselves. This past year I was given yet another new ad representative with no introduction. The paper has a large employee turnover in the ad department. The new ad representative's emails were sharp and short, giving me the impression that I was an unwanted interruption in his day. I was insulted and let him know it. He showed no concept of how to communicate by email to his customer. Remember, with email we still need to write in full sentences; we still need to show a bit of interest in the customer; and we still need to be polite.

Your email is a reflection of you and your company; therefore it should be well thought out, organized, and free from mistakes. There are times when email isn't sufficient and you must simply pick up the phone and call the person.

Some of my customers love to text me. When responding I have to make sure to edit and review before I send. Auto correct can just ruin my entire message. It's okay for the customer to misspell something or use the wrong verb but it's not okay for a business owner. We are supposed to be smarter and more professional than that. Again I remind you to review and edit text before you hit "send".

Websites

Technology is ever changing and for some of us it's difficult to keep up. However, most every business understands how critical it is to have a website. All businesses also need a mobile website, so make it part of your operation. Customers are searching for what they want and need on mobile devices. A recent survey showed 52% of local searches are done on mobile devices. In the past two years mobile search has grown five times. Smartphones and tablets are the main access point for the web. If you aren't real tech savvy or don't have time to build a mobile website, hire someone to do it for you.

Mobile devices also have the ability to handle payments in a quick fashion from almost anywhere. Depending on what you sell and how you conduct business mobile payment may be something you want to explore.

Make your mobile site and website neat and easy to navigate or people will move on to another business. Customers are always after convenience. Remember they have many choices of who to do business with so make it easy for them to choose you.

On both your traditional website and mobile site you can change your advertising or new product offerings weekly, monthly, or as often as you like. You will want to prominently display in the header or side bar social icons of sites where you have a presence so readers can easily follow you.

Social Networking

Social networking is the place to get a great deal of exposure. It's a low cost and direct line to prospective and current clients. Social networking can build relationships, keep you in touch with your customers, and build repeat and referral business. As with anything it takes time and energy. Start with one social site that you feel will benefit your business the most; Facebook, Pinterest, Twitter, and LinkedIn, are just a few suggestions.

Once you have an account and start posting on a site you will need to keep post regularly. People usually check their social sites every day. I have found that I get the most response... likes, comments, and shares from photos with a short quick description or title. With experience you will discover what works best for your business.

Marketing on Social Media

You can pay to advertise on social sites. I tried advertising on Facebook a couple of times, I did get a lot of response which was exciting, but no sales. Like any type of marketing you have to try it to see if it will work for you and your product or service. Most sites will have analytics for you to review.

Having a presence on other websites is a good way to build awareness and reach potential customers. If your suppliers have a website with a dealer locator feature you will definitely want to be included on their site. I have accounts with three national companies that have beautiful websites and a dealer locator feature on those sites. It cost me nothing but a little time to build a presence on their sites.

You may want to look into location based mobile advertising, text messaging mobile campaigns, and mobile web advertising. There are companies that can put together and execute ad campaigns for you if you have the budget for it and aren't inclined to do it yourself.

When you put together your annual budget remember to allocate for mobile devices and mobile advertising. If you aren't up on all the technology it can be overwhelming. If you feel overwhelmed, don't do what seems natural, which is to just ignore it and do nothing. Pay someone to do what you don't know how to do or pay someone to teach you.

PART THREE

Avoiding Miscommunication and Conflict

Chapter 17

Contracts, Terms, and Agreements

If we lived in a perfect world with perfect people, there wouldn't be a need for written contracts. But we don't live in a perfect world with perfect people. The reality is we must have written contracts or agreements to avoid confusion, conflicts, and misunderstandings.

An oral or written contract is an agreement between two or more people to do or not to do certain things. Once the contract is signed, it is legally binding. There may be exceptions; these can vary from state to state. Ask your lawyer or CPA about any exceptions concerning contracts.

The state of Virginia, which is where I live and work, allows the customer three days from the date of signing in which to cancel a contract if the customer was solicited by a company they have never done business with before and if the contract was written in the customer's home.

A written agreement can be as simple as a one-sheet contract, or it can be multiple pages. The length and complexity of a contract depends on the type of business, the size of the project, and the potential risk involved.

The main purposes of a written contract are clarification of what each person is getting and giving, plus legal protection. The Latin phrase *quid pro quo* means "something for something." That is why we need contracts—to make sure each party gets their "something" and is clear on what that something is. Contracts prevent most but not all miscommunication, misunderstanding, miscomprehension, legal battles, emotional upset, and damage to reputations. Specifics should be written into the contract, and I firmly believe the contract should be verbally presented to the customer for further clarity before it's signed.

A sensible, conscientious person watches for potential problems ahead and prepares to meet them, hoping they will not come. The fool never looks or plans for problems and suffers the consequences. Don't be a fool. Avoid miscommunication, which usually leads to problems.

EXAMPLE

Bly's Landscape Company had a sales appointment with Mrs. Mary Smith concerning landscaping her front yard. After much discussion, a contract was written, and Mrs. Smith signed it. The simple, straightforward contract basically read: Landscaping to be performed in Mrs. Mary Smith's front yard. Existing shrubs are to be removed, new shrubs to be supplied and planted for a cost of $5,000, and the work is to be completed within thirty days of the signed contract.

After the work was completed, the bill was presented to Mrs. Smith. The old shrubs had not been hauled away, and none of the new shrubbery had been mulched; therefore, she was unhappy. Bly's manager spoke with Mrs. Smith about the contract and pointed out that they had performed all work stated in the contract that she'd signed.

Why did Mrs. Smith think the old shrubs were to be hauled away and new mulch supplied if it wasn't in her contract? During the sales call, Bly's representative discussed removal of shrubs and applying new mulch, which did not fit into her budget. She remembered discussing those items and assumed she was getting everything they discussed.

Mrs. Smith's confusion and disappointment could have been avoided if Bly's sales representative had verbally gone over the contract, pointing out what Mrs. Smith was getting and the options she had declined because of her budget constraints.

Bly's manager wouldn't have had to explain the contract after the fact to Mrs. Smith or been put in an awkward situation if verbal communication during the sales process had been clearer. Nothing was wrong with the contract. It stated exactly what each person was giving and receiving.

During a sales call, so many options, products, and features are discussed that it's easy for the customer to become confused. Confusion, disappointment, and conflict do not promote repeat and referral business or assist in building a good reputation and relationship.

Be specific with your contracts; do not leave room for customer assumptions. Assumptions usually lead to negative reactions and feelings for all concerned. In your contract, be brand and quality specific if you offer different brand names and quality levels. Be number or quantity specific as well as specific about the work to be performed. Being specific prevents headaches and lost money.

EXAMPLE

I spent three hours in the home of a new customer discussing window treatment products and measuring and working up prices. She escorted me through rooms in her home to show me the windows she wanted treatments for. I wrote the contract and verbally went over it with her, and she accepted it. I thought the sale went very well; the customer was happy, and so was I. Three weeks later, my installer and I installed her treatments. When we were finished, she wanted to know where the rest of the window treatments were. Needless to say, I was confused. For some odd reason I have yet to figure out, she thought she was getting six more window treatments for two more rooms. I explained that I had never measured for window treatments in those two rooms because she hadn't shown those rooms to me. We hadn't discussed those rooms.

I had a copy of her contract with me, of course, so together we reviewed it. The contract was written with the name of each room, the number of window treatments for each of those rooms, the type of treatment, the brand name, and the color. She couldn't argue about the contract—it was all there in black and white with her signature. If I hadn't been specific, I would have been out the cost of six more window treatments. (Been there, done that.)

Because I am a professional and empathized with her, I apologized for the confusion, even though I had done nothing to confuse her. She appeared angry, and it was an uncomfortable situation for both of us. The contract protected me from financial loss, but not from emotional upset or the loss of a repeat customer.

Now, I go as far as to write my contracts stating whether a window treatment has a manual or automated control if I have discussed or shown both types of controls to the customer. Information overload during the sales process can cause the customer confusion and miscomprehension.

For a typical small business selling their services or products, a basic, straightforward contract is all that's needed. Of course, there are always exceptions; certain businesses may need industry-specific sections in their contracts.

Basic Information That Should be in All Contracts

- Company name and address
- Phone number
- Website
- Email
- Date
- Cancellation practices
- Customer name
- Estimated completion or delivery date
- Payment schedule
- Specific work to be performed
- Products and materials to be supplied
- Clause stating alteration or deviation procedures
- Signature line

At times, alterations or additions to the original contract may be necessary. Anytime there are changes, put in writing the additional work and supplies, plus the extra expense to the customer. Get the customer's signature <u>before</u> you begin the extra work. This is so you are protected. I have heard too many horror stories where the small businessperson was the victim of a greedy customer. The business did extra work the customer requested without an additional agreement to the original contract. Then the customer refused to pay, and the business owner had no legal recourse in getting paid.

Sometimes we get close to customers—they become our friends. When this happens, we get lax in writing contracts and agreement changes and in getting signatures. Put everything in writing. Don't leave anything to chance or you may be disappointed and financially taken advantage of once the job is completed.

Take the time to write your contract with all the details and specifics. I know it seems like extra work, and you may not want to do it. Do it anyway; either you or an employee can take charge of that responsibility. Make the contract or agreement a part of your business practice that requires the customer's signature before any work begins and before supplies or products are ordered. A detailed contract will save you money when a customer is confused, has misunderstood, has changed their mind, or is simply trying to take advantage of you.

I have included this simple, straightforward agreement that I use with my customers. This is just an example for you to see, not to adopt. You may need a more in-depth, industry-specific contract.

WINDOWS & WALLS

469 Whissens Ridge Road
Winchester, VA 22602
Phone # 540-877-2893   Fax # 540-877-1068
www.windows-and-walls.com

PROPOSAL

Date	Proposal #
12/18/2012	96

Description	Total
	0.00

Subtotal	$0.00
Sales Tax (5.0%)	$0.00
Total	$0.00

CUSTOM ORDERS MAY NOT BE CANCELLED. All work to be completed in a workman like manner according to standard practices. Any alteration or deviation from above specifications involving extra costs will be executed only upon written orders and will become an extra charge over and above the amount stated. All agreements contingent upon strikes, accidents or delays beyond our control. Windows & Walls shall have the right to make adjustments to achieve a reasonable fit. A down payment is required before order is processed. Balance is due upon installation.

SIGNATURE & DATE _____
acceptance of proposal, return one copy

Chapter 18

Misunderstandings and Conflicts

We all dread dealing with misunderstandings and conflicts—at least I do. Confrontation is not something I enjoy. I communicate clearly and specifically in conversations and in the written contract during the sales process to prevent any misunderstandings. Even so, misunderstandings happen once in a great while.

When a customer has misinterpreted what has been said or agreed upon after the fact, we have no choice but to deal with the situation. How we deal with the situation is up to us. Do you respond to this type of problem, conflict, or misunderstanding right away, or do you put it off? Responding to the misunderstanding immediately is usually the best approach, but not always the easiest. Sometimes we can't see any immediate profit in the effort we're going to put forth. Do yourself a favor: Make problems a priority and get them over with so they are off your mind. Quick action will build the customer's confidence in you greatly and prevent a potential crisis.

Quick response time is such a challenge for most small businesses. It seems that when a problem arises, becomes too difficult, or ventures out of the normal realm, the business (owner or employee) doesn't follow through. Quietly and conveniently, the customer and their problem are forgotten. You better believe the customer hasn't forgotten about his problem and he wants it addressed, taken care of, and corrected.

Responding quickly is to your advantage, because the longer you take to get back to your unhappy customer, the more agitated they become, and the more agitated they become, the more difficult they are to work with. A customer becomes agitated when they feel they're being avoided. If no one from the business has responded quickly (within twenty-four hours) to their complaint or concern, customers feel ignored or neglected. In any customer situation, take a second and imagine how you would feel if you were in their position. This always helps me to be more responsive and empathetic, and it should help you, too.

You may not be able to correct or resolve the problem immediately; you may not even know what the problem is. The point I am trying to get across is that you should respond, and respond immediately. Contact the customer, let them know you care, and let them know that you are willing to discuss whatever is bothering them. This is the first step in helping the customer feel more secure. At least they have talked to someone who is aware of their problem and willing to look into it.

Now that you're aware of the conflict, misunderstanding, problem, or whatever you want to call it, what do you do? There are steps to take, questions to be answered, information to gather, and behavior to adhere to before you can come up with a resolution.

First, you must know why the customer is unhappy. This can be a challenge in itself at times due to the customer's emotions, poor communication skills, or lack of knowledge about the product or service. When the customer is talking, do not interrupt. They need to vent and get all their frustrations or disappointments voiced. They will not hear a thing you say, anyway, until they can voice what's on their mind. They need to get whatever is bothering them off their mind; they need to vent before they can be open to what you are saying. Once they have voiced their issues, then and only then are they emotionally ready to hear what you have to say.

Some very important behaviors to follow are to stay calm, don't get defensive, don't say or act thoughtlessly, and don't make excuses. (At first this may take great effort and self-control.) This can be quite a challenge if the customer is upset and unreasonable. Stay calm and remember that you are in control. You are the one who must come up with a solution or answer to their issue. Our approach to problems is our decision. If we become defensive, the customer then reacts to our defensiveness, and things may escalate. Refrain from thoughtless actions and remarks; they are useless in helping you to resolve a problem.

Being right is overrated. Refrain from arrogantly pointing out to your customer that they are wrong and you are right. This action will not make the customer feel better—it will only make *you* feel better and superior. The customer will most likely be embarrassed and their pride will be bruised, which doesn't help to build good customer relationships.

You have been calm and maintained self-control while the customer voiced their issue. Now what do you do? Keep an open mind; do not assume you understand the issue or know the answer until you gather more information through questions, discussion, and review of the written contract or agreement. I don't know about you, but every time I assume I have the answer without all the information, I am wrong. It's very humbling.

Obtaining and reviewing all customer information will give you a clear picture of the true reason for the problem or misunderstanding. Once the reason for the misunderstanding is discovered, the resolution will be obvious. In addition to a careful review of the contract, you'll want to obtain information through private discussions with the customer, salesperson, workman, delivery personnel, and anyone else directly involved.

The following is information you need to know before you can offer a solution to a conflict or misunderstanding.

1. What is the customer's complaint, issue, or problem?
2. Once you feel you understand what the customer is concerned or unhappy about, confirm your understanding with them. Confirm by using a simple set of statements such as: "Mr. Dove, I want to be sure that I understand your concern (problem, issue, whatever word you want to

use). The concern is _____." This action does two things; it confirms to you what the customer's problem is, and it makes clear to the customer that you comprehend their problem.

3. Review all the details in the original signed contract, privately if possible. You need time to understand the contract without stress or pressure from someone looking over your shoulder. You will want to critically review the contract for any confusing or misleading wording.

4. Discuss the customer's job with any of your employees, subcontractors, or suppliers who were involved. Ask direct questions that pertain to the problem at hand to gain insightful information.

5. You need to know about the sales presentation: What items were shown, what was said, what was promised, or options discussed. A discussion with the salesperson is a must. If you made the sale, then you know what went on during the presentation and may remember what could have confused your customer.

Now that you have gathered the information, you can determine where the conflict or misunderstanding stemmed from and what can be done to resolve it.

EXAMPLE

I was out of the office one day when a customer called with a complaint. She said she was unhappy with the custom natural shade in her master bedroom because it was not lined, and she thought she ordered and paid for a lined shade.

I reviewed her contract and she was correct; she had ordered and paid for a lined shade. Next, I reviewed the shade manufacturer's invoice, and sure enough, I was charged for a lined shade. I called the installer and asked him if he noticed whether the shade had lining or not when he installed it. He did not remember.

After reviewing all the information, I called her back the same day she called me. I told her she was right. She had ordered and paid for a lined shade, and I would take care of the problem right away. I apologized for the mistake and the inconvenience.

Since I hadn't been on the installation, I had to inspect the shade to make sure it was not lined before I called the manufacturer about correcting the mistake. During the appointment to inspect the shade, the customer wanted to know why there was a mistake and how was it going to be handled. At this point I knew where the mistake lay, but not exactly how it would be corrected. I said that it was human error on the part of the manufacturer, and that they would either replace it or take the original one back to have the lining installed—it was the manufacturer's decision. I told her I would call her in a day or two at the latest to inform her of how and when the problem would be resolved.

To correct the mistake, I called the manufacturer and explained the problem. They realized it was their error and said they would replace the entire shade, and that it would take about two weeks to ship. I then called the customer and relayed the information.

Once the shade was delivered to me it had to be taken to the customer's home. The existing one had to be removed, the new one installed, and the original one packed up and shipped back to the manufacturer. Again I apologized to her for all the inconvenience. She thanked me for taking care of the problem so quickly, and she mentioned a future project.

You can see by the above example that a lot of time and effort goes into tracking down the origin of a problem before you can resolve it. I gathered the information, called the customer, apologized, inspected the problem personally, followed through on resolving the problem, and took care of the customer. Problems cost us time, effort, money, and worry. How we resolve a problem and how quickly we resolve it can mean the difference between a good or poor business reputation and whether we have continual repeat and referral business.

**Guidelines and Questions to Assist
You in Forming the Best Solutions**

1. Be aware of how your emotions may influence your solution.
2. Consider how your solution may affect your customer and your business.
3. Weigh and evaluate the costs of time, money, energy, worry, reputation, and future business associated with the various solutions.
4. Is the solution fair to your customer?
5. Will the solution resolve the problem in a reasonable amount of time?
6. Is the solution a long-term or short-term answer to the problem?
7. Will the solution keep you in good standing with the customer?
8. Is it important for you to keep this customer?

Now that you know how to uncover the facts and information pertaining to a problem, what's next? Deciding on the best solution is the next step.

Keep in mind that no two situations or customers are the same; therefore, the solutions and interactions will never be the same. At times the solution to a problem is obvious: It's an easy fix and oh, how relieved we are when that's the case. Other times, we have more difficult problems to contend with that require more effort and skill.

Now that you have the facts and the solution, how do you present the solution to your customer? Depending on the magnitude of the problem, you may want to make an appointment and meet the customer face to face to discuss the solution. If it's something fairly simple and easy to correct, a phone call or email to discuss things may be all that's necessary.

Guidelines for Presenting Your Solution

1. Take responsibility.
2. Apologize again for the inconvenience.
3. Be pleasant.
4. Be empathetic.
5. Don't talk too much or use language that confuses your customer.
6. Make sure your body language is relaxed.
7. Present your solution to the problem, stay focused, and don't sway from the problem.
8. Give the customer time (a few minutes) to comprehend the solution and respond. In other words, after you offer a solution, be quiet so they can think.
9. Encourage questions.

Once your customer has accepted the solution, inform them of the time frame and any extra costs they may incur. Give them the necessary information needed, but do not bog them down with confusing details and jargon.

What if the customer doesn't accept the solution you offered? As long as you and the customer are on good terms, more discussion may be necessary. Since your solution was not acceptable to them, ask what they suggest. This does not mean you have to do what they suggest, but by asking the question you get an answer that lets you know what they want. Hopefully, through communication you can come to a mutual agreement without any hard feelings.

If the customer is being unreasonable in accepting your solution and you know without a doubt you are being fair and have complied with the contract, then an ultimatum may be necessary. You might have to say something such as, "I have complied with the contract and offered a fair solution to the problem. Take some time to think about it. If you still don't want to accept this fair and reasonable solution, I guess we have no choice but to let our lawyers work this out."

Sometimes the reality of lawyers, court, time, emotional upset, and money will bring people to their senses. Give the customer a few days to think things over.

Often, after attaining all the facts, we realize the customer is confused about what they bought, or they misunderstood the contract. We know the customer is <u>NOT</u> always right. How do we handle this situation? We do it carefully and tactfully. Again, there are guidelines to help us through this delicate process.

Guidelines to Handle Misunderstandings

- Talk to the customer face to face.
- Choose your words carefully.
- Apologize sincerely about the confusion or misunderstanding.
- Do not use a condescending or accusatory tone.
- Bring up what you believe they misunderstood and discuss it.
- Go over the contract together; sometimes this exercise alone will clear things up.
- Review what they are unhappy or confused about.
- Discuss what they want in order to be satisfied.
- Be diplomatic and try to see their side.
- Offer a solution both of you can live with.

If the solution involves further investment on their part, you will have to address it now. Do not assume they *know* this is going to cost them more money. Do not present them with a surprise bill after the problem is taken care of—that's bad business.

Some customers aren't reasonable or realistic; some are just impossible to please, and believe me, I have had my share of them over the past twenty-eight years. If you're in business for any length of time, you will have your fair share of difficult or communication-challenged customers, too. You will have war stories to share with other business owners.

Weigh the benefits of compromise against the cost of crossing the customer. You may decide it's better to take a small loss of time and money than upset a customer. If the customer is influential and could damage your reputation, then you may want to do whatever it takes to make them happy. We all take our lumps in the business world.

Weigh the long-term pros and cons of satisfying your customer, even though you know the fault lies with them. I make this suggestion purely for monetary reasons, even though it appears otherwise.

EXAMPLE

A husband and wife selected a new kitchen countertop to replace the old one in their home. They purchased it from a big box store. After it was installed, the wife didn't like it. She convinced herself and her husband that it was not the countertop they selected—that it was one of many they had looked at with the store associate, but not their final decision.

They were unhappy with the countertop and made a big issue of it, even though the order they placed and signed had the name and color of the exact countertop they received. To their delight, the store replaced the countertop at no extra cost to them. These customers have since purchased many large appliances from this store. I doubt they would have stayed loyal to the store had it not replaced the countertop.

The store invested a small amount of money to keep the customers happy. In the long term, the investment paid off because the customers continued to do business there

In small business misunderstandings there are at least two parties involved: The customer and the business. The business carries the responsibility when it comes to communication, meeting its contractual agreements, and problem solving. In correcting or smoothing out a misunderstanding, the business owner or key employee must respond quickly to the customer. Procrastination agitates the problem further.

As business problems and miscommunications have popped up over the years I have learned valuable lessons, hard and uncomfortable but valuable. I didn't always want to learn a lesson; privately I blamed the problem on my unreasonable customer and felt sorry for myself. In time, after my pride healed, I always learned something and grew from the experience.

From and through my customers I have learned lessons in human nature, customer relationships, approach, business, patience, professionalism, and life. Sometimes I made the mistake, sometimes the customer was at fault, but no matter, I always learned a lesson. These lessons always come with costs of money, time, effort, and pride.

If you're not learning from your problems, you really do have a problem. Don't believe your excuses. Step back, increase your awareness, put your ego aside, and see what went wrong and why. It may not be anything you did wrong but something additional you need to do. Learn how to look for possible problems ahead and prepare either to avoid or meet them.

A change in procedures may be needed to prevent problems from occurring. Sometimes we have been doing a thing the same way for so long that we can't see it needs improvement. When we keep doing the same thing in the same way and are not satisfied with the results, then we need to change ourselves or the way we do things. We suffer the consequences if we don't prepare for change and problems.

CHAPTER 19

Knowing When to Let a Customer Go and How

Letting a customer go is never an easy decision or a pleasant task. The phrase "firing the customer" is popular and catchy today, but a bit harsh.

As business owners, we think we need and want all customers. Most of the time that's true, but every now and then a customer is more trouble than they're worth. If you have a customer who is always unreasonable, demanding, demeaning, or just plain crazy, they can make you miserable. They can drain the life and enthusiasm out of you and use up so much of your emotional and mental energy that you have very little left for anything or anyone else.

When a customer continually makes you miserable or is constantly on your mind, it might be time to let them go. I'm not saying you should let every customer go who is demanding or hard to please. I'm talking about the absurdly demanding—the customer, who causes you to lose sleep, promotes ulcers, saps all of your energy, or makes you feel as if you're a servant. Consider letting them go.

Don't get rid of a customer when you're angry or emotionally upset. It's best to wait until you've cooled down and can rationally make a decision.

Once you've set your emotions aside, ask yourself the following questions. Your answers will guide you to the correct decision.

QUESTIONS

1. Is the customer demeaning to you or your employees?
2. Is the customer taking up too much time for the return?
3. Does the customer change their mind often?
4. Is the customer disrespectful to you or your employees?
5. Are their expectations unrealistic?
6. Are they constantly complaining about your service, products, or prices?
7. Do they often miss appointments?
8. Do you constantly have to change your schedule for them?
9. Is their behavior unusual in the sense that they are in an altered state due to alcohol or drugs? (If so, they may not remember their decisions.)
10. Can your business financially afford to lose this customer?
11. Are you truly justified in letting this customer go?
12. Are you being too sensitive?
13. Are you being rational?
14. Have you or your employees done or said something to cause the customer to be difficult?

After you've answered the questions above, list what the customer has done or said that causes you to want to get rid of them. If you can't put what they've done down on paper … well, maybe it's not all the customer. This exercise is for your eyes only.

Once you've decided to let the customer go, how do you do it in a professional way? I think it best to tell the customer either in person or on the phone, but if you just can't bring yourself to do that, a letter will suffice. Do not inform them by text or email.

Keep the conversation or letter short, to the point, and unemotional. Always strive to be kind and professional in all communication. The box below contains a few short examples of how to let a customer go.

EXAMPLES

Due to the differences in our personalities I feel it best for you to consider using another service. Thank you for your past business.

At this time I am so busy I think it is to your advantage to seek out another company to fill your needs. Thank you.

You will benefit by using a company that offers more of what you are looking for. My company can't meet all of your needs at this time. Thank you for your consideration.

It appears we are unable to satisfy your demands. Therefore, we will not be available for future service to you. Thank you for your past business.

I have had many customers over the years that I would like to have given to my competitors. I felt and thought I had to take care of all customers and put up with their behavior. For some of us it's difficult to say no.

One time I let a customer go, and I have never regretted it. I had decorated five rooms in this young woman's home over a two-year period. She was a demanding customer, always wanting unusual, over-the-top designs. The end results were always stunning, and she was always happy with the final outcome.

Her living room was the last decorating project we were working on. Every design and fabric I presented she disliked. Nothing pleased her. None of my suggestions appealed to her, and she really didn't know what she wanted. After four or five (I don't remember now) appointments, I was exhausted with her demands and very busy with other customers.

I didn't let her go because she didn't like my ideas and suggestions. I let her go because she was wasting too much of my time. She was not ready to commit to her decorating project, and my other customers were not getting the attention they required or deserved.

How I let this customer go was not planned but a spur of the moment decision, which I do not recommend to anyone. She called about her living room, and once again after considering my recommendations did not like anything. She could hear the disappointment and exasperation in my voice. At this point she said, "I know I take a lot of energy and time. I can hear the frustration in your voice. Maybe you should take a couple of days to decide if you want to work with me." It was a knee-jerk reaction on my part that I've never regretted, but I told her, "I don't need a couple of days to think about it. You're right—I'm very busy and a little stressed with all the work I have right now. You should find someone else who has more time to work with you."

I felt so relieved after I hung up the phone. It was a liberating feeling to not have to put together one more design to be shot down yet again. I wonder if her living room ever got completed.

CHAPTER 20

Conclusion

Owning and running a small business requires a great deal from the owner, especially in the early years. It takes time, planning, and dedication to customers, employees, and the industry one is in. Running a successful business requires continual education in one's field, hard work, honesty, difficult decision making, risk taking, long hours, sacrifice, and the willingness to do what needs to be done. There is no room for the attitude "that's not my job."

A small business owner must take responsibility for just about everything their business supplies, sells, does, and offers. A portion of our pride, self-respect, and ego are on the line with every customer we come in contact with, every job we do, and every decision we make. If our business is small enough, <u>we are the business</u> to our customers.

Our hopes and dreams are wrapped up in our business. Eventually, just about everything important to us depends on the success of our business. How can that be?

We start a small business because we have a dream or an ambition to do something different, or to do something on our own. Being our own boss and doing things our way appeals to us. Our business is our idea and as such is an extension of our creative self.

Conclusion

Unless you are a trust fund baby or financially well off, you will need an income. We all need an income. We have to make a living and bring home a paycheck so the bills get paid.

If you're a business owner, you most likely have ambition, drive, dreams, and desires. You desire more than just enough money to get by. Maybe you want to take exotic vacations, save for your children's college, live in a bigger house, drive a nicer car, put in a swimming pool, or retire early. Whatever the specifics, you want more than just enough money to squeak by on year after year. You want a better life for yourself and your family, and you plan on attaining it through your successful small business.

The success of your small business is critical for your present life situation and critical for your future and the future of your loved ones. Lifestyle, higher education, comfort, retirement, good health insurance, travel, dreams, and desires are wrapped up in your success with your small business.

So you see most of your hopes and your family's hopes, dreams, and future are wrapped up in the success of your business.

Next is a list of fifty qualities, abilities and skills that propel every business owner to success. You possess many of these already, I'm sure. A great business is not built on one quality or activity alone, but by doing many things well time and time again. Many problems can be avoided and your business can run smoother if you develop these qualities and skills. Work on building one skill or quality every couple of weeks until it's a habit, then add another. Trying to develop all of these qualities at the same time is overwhelming; just take one at a time.

FIFTY QUALITIES

1. Awareness
2. Ability to delegate
3. Asking for help when needed
4. Flexibility
5. Control of your negative emotions
6. Confidence
7. Exceptional communication skills
8. Basic knowledge and understanding of record keeping
9. Curiosity
10. Diplomacy
11. Consideration of advice given by others
12. Desire for success
13. Detail oriented
14. Empathy for others
15. Forgiveness
16. Follow up
17. Follow through
18. Honesty
19. Integrity
20. Leadership
21. Ability to say no when necessary
22. Prioritize work
23. Insight
24. Time management
25. Realize you don't know it all
26. Strive to lead a balanced life
27. Stretch past your comfort zone
28. Apologize sincerely
29. Willingness to do what needs doing
30. Sense of humor
31. Understanding of others
32. Pleasant personality
33. Sense of fairness
34. Tolerance of others

35. Reasoning skills
36. Self discipline
37. Delayed gratification
38. Problem solving skills
39. Critical thinking skills
40. Self motivation
41. Organizational skills
42. Sense of urgency
43. Respect for others
44. Develop consistency
45. Trust yourself
46. Build a good team
47. Take responsibility
48. Be accountable
49. Set yearly, monthly, and weekly business goals
50. Keep things simple (which means not complicated)

Throughout this book I have discussed repeat and referral business, customer service, and communication. All this knowledge is useless unless you apply it. Even if you only apply two or three of the principals in this book, it will increase your chance of financial success.

What gives a small business its life, its momentum, and its reputation? People! People give small business its life and momentum plus build its reputation. Owners, managers, and employees bring life to every business with their energy, skills, knowledge, passion, creativity, and drive. A product, an idea, or a concept alone can't cause anything to happen. It takes people to make things happen.

You are creative; you have the energy to cause things to happen, both good and bad. You have the ability to make a successful business that's both financially and personally rewarding, so do it. Go after it.

I wish you the greatest of success and the best future!

ABOUT THE AUTHOR

Judy Day Wilfong is founder and president of New Vision Windows and Walls Inc., a decorating business that specializes in custom window treatments. For 28 years and counting she has managed her successful business in the beautiful Shenandoah Valley, in Winchester, Virginia. She is a highly respected business owner.

Judy has won many national design competitions and business awards throughout the years. Her designs have been featured in several trade magazines during her design career. One of the premier national interior fashions trade magazines featured an article on her design business.

She has also served as business advisor and teacher to many other small business owners throughout the United States due to her experience and practical, common-sense approach to business.

Judy graduated cum laude from Lord Fairfax Community College and was honored with the Outstanding Graduate award. She lives in Winchester Virginia with her husband.

Judy is available to give business advice or for consultation. If you would like her to speak at an event you're hosting, please address all correspondence to:

Judy Wilfong
469 Whissen's Ridge Road
Winchester Virginia 22602
E-mail: Judy@JudyWilfong.com
www. JudyWilfong.com   .